Book 1

Because It's There:

To Climb Mount Everest

Because It's There:
To Climb Mount Everest

A Memoir

By Aleksey Berzon

Acknowledgments

This book would not have been possible without the dedication of everyone at the Daytona Beach Writing Group and Ormond Writers' League (OWLs). They have inspired me to start the book and guided me to become the writer that I am today.

Warmest regards to the hardworking and calming influence of Barbara Richford, Group President of the Daytona Beach Writing Group. Her unending support and creative ideas helped me complete the book. Group Vice President Patty Hoffmann's talent and critical eye for details made all things seem possible. A special thanks to my fellow members for their guidance: Frank Farmer, Mary Lee Croatt, Connie Storch, Cheri Wine, Sarah Carlson Ditmyer and others. Thank you all! (I know I broke the apostrophe rule ☺.)

Ormond Writers' League will always have my gratitude for their insightful support during my time with them: Lorraine Ruhl, Diana Zimmerman, Veronica Hart and everyone else. Thank you all!

Charles Stoll's eye for detail and guidance with scene description has helped me immensely. Sam Cromartie's gift with action scenes and keeping the story moving inspired me to do the same. Thank you Sam!

Big thanks to Taylor Duck for her support, unending enthusiasm and desire to read the completed book. She helped me to push on with the last few difficult steps to self-publish my work.

Peggy Holloway is an inspiration to me. Her successful writing career and adamant belief in keeping her own voice helped me not to lose myself in the boundless world of writing styles. She has opened my eyes to the possibility of self-publishing and helped guide the way.

Finally, I owe the greatest amount of gratitude to Nepal and all the people who helped make my Mount Everest journey.

Without them, I wouldn't have a story. Thank you everyone!

About the Author

Aleksey Berzon has been a teacher, outdoor education instructor, merchant marine, and a master naturalist. He has climbed Mount Everest, survived an airplane crash and taught kids at a remote Buddhist monastery in the Himalayas.

He resides in Palm Coast, Florida and works as an International Tour Director. In his free time, Aleksey travels to remote destinations around the world with his backpack, compass, tent, and a sleeping bag seeking adventure and unique cultures.

All of Mr. Berzon's books are available on amazon.

Amazon Books Keyword: Aleksey Berzon

Aleksey Berzon books may be purchased for educational, business, or sales promotional use.

For information, please email: wintrol84@hotmail.com

Photos are only included in the ebook version, not paperback.

Italicized words are further explained in the glossary at the end of the book.

Currency Exchange Rate and Metric Conversion

1 Kilometer = 0.62 Miles

1 Mile = 1.61 Kilometers

1 Meter = 3.28 Feet

1 US Dollar = 84 Nepalese Rupee (Year 2013)

1 US Dollar = 6.1 Chinese Yuan (Year 2013)

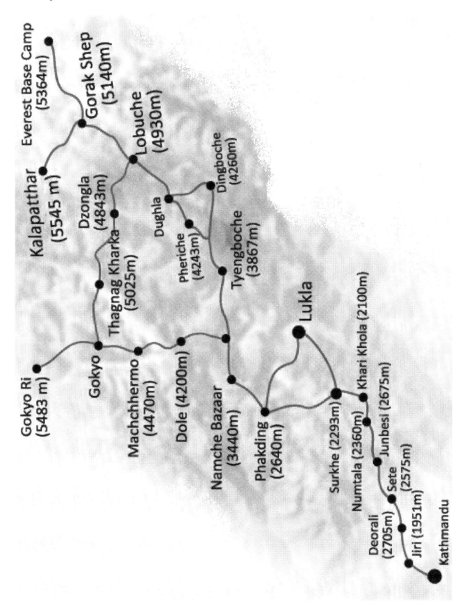

Table of Contents

Part 1

The Beginning

Chapter 1

The winds screamed more than howled. Rain fell as stones. The trees swayed and moaned, and branches tore like paper limbs. This storm, more ferocious than any other in my memory, raged on like drums on a battlefield. Yet with every passing moment, I worried more about my connecting flight to Nepal than destruction caused by the *hurricane*. My journey depended on it.

I looked out the window and felt the gusts of wind pummel the twelve-story building where I stayed. Trash bins and plastic bags flew about the playground as I looked down from the tenth floor. The storm showed no sign of abating. The date was October 29, 2012, the very day Hurricane Sandy made landfall in New York City with gusts of wind over eighty miles-per-hour.

"It's good your flight was cancelled. I know you can't wait to start your adventure in China and Nepal, but your safety is more important," my grandmother said in Russian as she relaxed in a recliner with a book in her lap.

I sighed. "Yes, Grandma. I agree. But why did Hurricane Sandy have to hit the same day as my flight? And I only have three days to make my connecting flight." I continued to watch the destruction unfold outside.

~*~*~

The morning of October 30, Hurricane Sandy rampaged on and showed no visual signs of ending. I checked Google news for a possibility of the *JFK International Airport* reopening. Mayor *Michael Bloomberg* made the headlines as he declared Sandy to be the "Storm of The Century." The time to evacuate was over.

In other popular news, I read, "*Ground Zero* Is Flooding" and below that "Sharks Swimming in Subway Sparks Fear." How devastating. Yet, on the other hand, hurricanes, sharks and subways could make an excellent *B movie*.

~*~*~

JFK International Airport reopened on October 31, and the first and only flight to China departed. Needless to say, I wasn't on it. Everyone with scheduled flights who didn't make it were placed on a waiting list until further notice.

As much as I loved New York City, my journey couldn't begin until I was on a plane to China. After a two-hour telephone conversation with *Air China*, I was told that the earliest available flight would depart November 8.

My hopeless attempt to bump up the departure date had failed, and I decided on a more direct approach. I would take the matter into my own hands and talk to the airline company in person. I followed the simple rule of standing up one time more than I got knocked down.

~*~*~

Apparently, I was not the only person who had the idea to take matters into their own hands. On November 1, people crowded the airport check-in lobby. Families with excess luggage took every available space and made a line that stretched past the exit doors and continued outside.

A family behind me stayed so close I smelled their sweat. The line in front had not budged for the past hour. Two men to my right shouted, pushed and shoved. Only one would claim the spot in front. Despite the loud scene, security only glanced and did not intervene.

The next six hours, I saw people fight and cry. Families were separated due to limited airplane seating. The emotional scenes shook my adamant belief in getting the earliest flight. Was I right to take a seat from a child who might be separated from a parent?

Who knew the situation that awaited them at their destination, and the effects Hurricane Sandy had on their lives? After all, this was only a vacation for me, but then again, it seemed more like a lifestyle. My cold-hearted choice had to be made. I was not responsible for their lives and choices.

When my turn finally arrived, I was not hopeful but determined. To my surprise, Air China found me a departing flight within several hours. The benefits of being a solo traveler started to show. So, there I sat, on my way to China, finally. An airplane filled with people, who, like me, endured Hurricane Sandy in New York City.

Chapter 2

As I thought back on the past year of tireless work assignments, it dawned on me that I've envisioned this moment countless times. When work overwhelmed me, the thought of starting this journey helped relieve stress and gave me purpose to push on.

I glanced around the airplane cabin and enjoyed the atmosphere. I loved the long, twelve to fourteen-hour flights, not the short domestic flights that have the uncomfortable seats and lack meals.

The flight time was my time. No one could reach me on the telephone and everything else would wait until I landed. For the next fourteen hours, I could be as lazy as I wanted, without feeling an ounce of guilt. In fact, laziness was not only accepted but encouraged. To remain seated at all times with the seatbelt buckled.

I could watch the newly released movies until I passed out due to lack of sleep and nap anytime I wanted just because there was nothing better to do. And the best part of the long flights was the convenience to order seconds of the delicious airplane food.

To prove my point, I waved to the passing flight attendant. "Excuse me, may I please have another serving of food? I'm still hungry."

She smiled. "Would you like chicken or salmon?"

"Salmon, please," I answered, admiring her customer service skills. Her bright smile reminded me of my countless work flights within the United States. American flight attendants often frowned and gave me the evil eye, as if I'd asked for the last piece of bread from a starving child instead of a tiny bag of pretzels.

"You sure like to eat," my seatmate commented.

Her expression showed a look surprise and anticipation rather than judgment.

"I sure do. I am trying to fatten up as much as I can, and the food here is delicious. Air China has not yet been corrupted by strict regulations and tight budget restrictions, unlike the good ole United States. I'll be ordering a few more lunches until the flight ends."

"This is the first time I've heard of someone wanting to gain weight. You think the food in China will be that bad? Or are you training for a food eating competition?"

It felt refreshing to hear the woman's frankness. "That's funny you say that. I actually entered several food eating competitions and won. Most people think they can just show up hungry and have a chance to win the tournament, but like any competition, training is essential for success. Would you like to know a secret? It's a way to stretch the stomach so you can put more food in it?" I smiled.

She laughed. "I need to know how to make my stomach smaller not bigger, but go ahead and tell me. I'll at least know what not to do."

"Sure. You do this for breakfast. Drink lots of water, then afterwards eat nothing but plain, white bread. The bread will absorb the water in the stomach and expand. It'll stretch it. Do this for a week and it's temporary. Do this for a month or longer, the effects will be more lasting. It works wonders."

She paused for a moment. "After hearing this, I'll have to re-think my breakfast options. My name is Alice."

I studied her long, brown hair, tied in a single ponytail, and thought her age to be around forty. "Nice to meet you, Alice. My name is Aleksey. Call me Alex if that's easier for you. Why are you going to China?"

"I am in the process of adopting a child. It's taking me a lot longer to get the paperwork done, but it's worth it. And you still haven't answered the reason for your desire to gain weight."

"Wow. I wish you success, and may this be the last trip you need to make before adoption. As for me, I need to gain weight before my attempt to climb Mount Everest. I've done little preparation due to a respiratory infection for the past three months. I might as well start preparing now by gaining some natural food reserves."

As if on cue, the flight attendant replaced my food tray.

"Did you say Everest? And you didn't prepare for it? You stupid or something?"

Despite the harsh words, she seemed concerned.

I smiled. "I know it's not the smartest thing to do, but Everest was not even in my plans until a month ago. It was the change of Chinese visa laws, at the last moment, and my love for mountains that led me here. And besides, I have enough experience to know when to turn back during the climb."

"Well, I don't know what to say to that. Good luck. What changed with the visa laws?"

"A lot. It used to be easy but not anymore. Due to the 2012 Chinese presidential elections, new visa regulations were introduced. This made my three-month journey to China impossible. The law required an exact date of entry and departure along with a full, prepaid itinerary of my visit. In other words, all hotels and attractions for the three months had to be prepaid and dated.

"I tried going to several travel agencies, but they weren't helpful and cost too much. In the end, I realized that I made things too difficult. Since I already had an entry flight to China, I only needed to make a departing flight a day after. I looked at the nearby countries with the cheapest flights and chose Nepal. Since Everest is in Nepal, I decided to climb it." I paused for a moment and remembered the desperate attempts I'd made to get the visa.

"That's quite the story. So, what inspired you to take such risks? Going to faraway places and all," Alice asked and sipped her steaming cup of *green tea*.

"Traveling is my passion, my hobby and my job. Everest was always on my bucket list, but I didn't expect it to come so soon. What inspired me? I don't know. Maybe because some of my best memories were made when I ventured into the unknown.

I had my backpack, a tent, sleeping bag, food, a compass and I just went. There was no plan, no itinerary, sometimes not even a destination.

"I picked a mountain or a remote village and made it my destination. I struggled there regardless of the pain, hunger, sickness or anything. It didn't matter. There was only the goal. I put my life on the line for this. It may not have made any sense to others, but at the time, it was the only thing that mattered to me."

Alice put down the cup and gave me her full attention. "Aren't you afraid of getting lost, or running out of food and water?"

I enjoyed talking about myself and gladly shared. "Yes, sometimes. That's why I push myself to where I can only go forward. I want to know how far I can go. Only then can I discover my limits, physical and otherwise. I think this is the reason I can't find a travel partner. They must always have a safety net, a nine-one-one *satellite phone* and can never take a chance on the uncertain. They always back out halfway. How will they ever know how far they can go without even trying?" I raised my voice at the question.

Frustration overwhelmed me as I recalled memories of the past. In particular, several travel partners who seemed excited at the beginning but backed out after a day of venturing into the unknown.

"Too dangerous," they all claimed the journey to be, and then turned back to the safety of a modern-day trail with the convenience of a coffee shop at every corner. Sure, I stereotyped them, but these memories weren't far from the truth.

After a short pause, I continued. "When I ventured without looking back, I learned so much. I found out what my body and mind were capable of. Sometimes I ended up pushing myself past the limit and grew stronger. Other times, I broke down halfway but damn, I tried. And no matter how bad the situation got, something good always happened in the end.

"I met amazing people who helped me, found better routes

or ended up making life-memorable adventures. And the best part, I had no regrets. I looked back at my failures and saw them as accomplishments. Regardless, whether I succeeded or failed, I felt freer at that moment than any planned itinerary could ever offer. I agree with the idiom, 'The greater the risk, the greater the reward.'" I stopped talking and reflected.

Alice nodded. "I love adventures too, although I prefer my coffee shops and a warm bed at the end of the day. I worry more about the people. The nature is beautiful, but people are not always so."

"You're right, Alice. However, please don't let these thoughts stop you from taking chances with strangers as you travel. I know I've been lucky on past trips. Maybe because I believe I can read situations well, but people are generally good. Some of the fondest memories I've had started with a simple conversation with a random individual on the road.

"Although, it's easier to socialize with locals when I travel alone. I'm more approachable this way. On every past adventure, I've been invited to someone's home and met their family. It's the best way to experience the local culture. I've learned to cook traditional dishes, rode horses, better understood the country's political situation or simply stayed for the night. When I first started traveling, I worried about—"

"About the cost of their kindness?" Alice finished my sentence.

I laughed. "Sometimes, but more so of burdening them. I was concerned that I took more than I could give back. That I took too much from a family, which had so little. But I was wrong. Eventually, I realized people invited me to stay at their home, not so much for me, but for themselves.

"For them, it was fun to meet a foreigner like me, especially an American touring a remote village. They often enjoyed my visit as much as I did and bragged about it to all their neighbors. I know because half of the time my hosts called their neighbors and partied as if it were 1699, with biscuits, tea and a conversation.

"At the end, I always gave the family some money. The funny part is that the husbands usually refused my money. Their wives, on the other hand, were more open to the idea and gladly took what I offered."

I looked around and realized I had talked too long. Most of the passengers had submitted their empty lunch plates and started getting ready for a nap.

Alice didn't seem to mind my talking and continued with, "My biggest fear is arriving to a foreign country where no one speaks English. What do you do when the other people don't speak the language?"

"Sometimes, I sit at a table filled with people who don't speak English. The atmosphere can get awkward quickly. I've learned to carry postcards with me. I take them out and everyone at the table comes over to glance at my home, at America. I show them my city, my beach and my house from an aerial view. It's the perfect ice breaker. I'm no longer a stranger but an individual with a story. Postcards also make for an excellent gift." I sighed. "Sorry. I've talked too much. I seem to be in a talkative mood today."

"It's OK. I've enjoyed listening to your stories." She smiled.

"Thank you." I chuckled. "Can I share one more story with you? Hopefully, this will offer a conclusion as to why I travel the way I do."

"Ready, set, go." Alice waved her hand energetically as if she were starting a race.

"Several years back I spent over two months walking a pilgrimage in Japan. There I met Kato, a Japanese man, who also walked the same trail. We journeyed together and became friends. One night, we found free accommodations in a tiny one-room cabin at a *Buddhist temple*.

"I still remember that night clearly. Kato sat in a corner failing to warm up a bowl of noodles using his small backpacker canister stove. I stood at the other corner and tried to clean a dirty blanket I wanted to use for the night. At that moment, I couldn't help but ask, 'Kato, you are a respected businessman and can stay at the best hotel and eat at a restaurant of your choice. Why are you here with me? Why do you go through all this discomfort?'

"Kato turned to look at me and returned a genuine smile of contentment and happiness. He then said the words I'll never forget. 'At home, I have family waiting for me. I have a job, friends and most comforts that money can offer. In order to appreciate the life I have at home, I am here to experience a different way of life. Wait. No.' Kato paused for a moment. 'I travel to live a different life.' He nodded as if agreeing with his own philosophy.

"He then glanced at me, and asked, 'Why are you doing this pilgrimage?' I couldn't answer Kato on the spot, but the next morning after we parted ways, I understood. I also traveled to live a different life."

I glanced at Alice. She was eating a small bag of potato chips. "Where did you get that?" I pointed to the bag.

"I decided I didn't need to watch the 'idiot box' also known as television. Listening to your stories is just as entertaining." She glanced at her *Lay's Classic* potato chip bag. "Too bad I don't have popcorn."

I smiled. "You're funny. You know, I just realized that Alice was the very first hurricane in the United States to have a name. Since 1953, all hurricanes had female names."

"Well, tickle me silly. No wonder my teacher called me 'Hurricane Alice.' And there I thought it was because of my outgoing personality. Why were women named after all those disasters? That's so sexist."

"I have no idea but that changed in 1979. Hurricane Bob was the first hurricane to have a man's name."

"Poor Bobs around the world. What have they done to deserve this?"

I laughed. "You know, I think this will be a fun flight."

After an hour of heartfelt talk, I took out my travel journal and wrote down our conversation in detail. I made it a habit to write down the day's events. Far in the future, I planned to write a book about my travels, the interesting people I'd met and the occasional thoughts of a wanderer.

Chapter 3

During the last hour of the flight, cabin crew handed out customs forms. My lack of research about the process worried me. By the time I filled out the forms, I felt the bump from the tires hit the runway. I had officially arrived in China.

Alice and I wished each other good luck and parted ways.

When I exited the airplane, I saw "Customs" written on a sheet of paper taped to a wall. Below the sign, an arrow pointed the way.

Chinese *customs* were surprisingly quick and efficient. No useless questions, not even a sidelong glance of suspicion directed at me. The simple, standard procedure included an entry stamp, collection of luggage, and then exiting to the main terminal.

After finishing the process, I stood in the middle of the *Shanghai Pudong International Airport* with a confused look on my face.

"Now what?" I spoke aloud as if an answer would magically appear.

I had to make a decision whether to go into the city center and stay at a *hostel* or spend the night at the airport to catch a connecting flight to Chengdu, China, early morning. My concern of a limited budget won. I decided to spend the night at the airport.

I usually didn't mind sleeping in airports. Lobby seats were comfortable enough. Alternatively, if the airport allowed it, sleeping on the floor was fine too. My *Therm-A-Rest*, a backpacker inflatable mattress, worked perfectly as a makeshift bed.

Despite my lax attitude toward sleeping arrangements, I still had standards. I had to be away from heavy walking traffic and near a power outlet, within reach, to recharge my telephone. In addition, I hoped others slept nearby. Then I wouldn't attract attention.

After I found a location that met all three of these conditions, I sat down on a plastic chair, placed the backpack in front of me and put my legs on top of it. Adapting to the situation was important.

Having hours of free time, I practiced Chinese. I hadn't dedicated much time to learning the language beforehand. Instead, I prepared a notepad with fifteen essential words. I had them printed in Chinese along with an English translation. This way if my pronunciation wasn't understood, I'd point to the printed words. The most important phrase being, "How much?"

As I studied the Chinese phrases, a man sitting a few seats away asked me a question in English, "Studying Chinese?"

He surprised me. I turned and studied the man. He looked middle aged, dark skinned, balding and wore a casual, unkempt business suit, badly wrinkled. "Yeah, it's a difficult language, but I'll get it eventually."

"Chinese is impossible, and by far, the hardest language. I've been coming to China for seven years now, and I still have difficulty saying the words correctly. You have an accent. Where are you from?"

I thought about his question and felt more comfortable being a Russian rather than an American. "I'm from Russia."

"But you have an accent. You sound more American than Russian. I talk to many Russian people, and your English is great."

I felt pressured by his directness and went on the defensive. "Yeah, I went to school in the United States, learned the language and now I live there. Where are you from?" I tried to change the subject.

"I am from Iran, a business man. I hope you don't mind me asking about your origin. My work requires me to talk to people, and now it's a hobby of mine to figure out where people are from."

He continued, "I like Russia. It's a great country and has good people. Although, sometimes it can be difficult to make a deal, but nothing that a bottle of vodka can't solve. I've been to Russia many times, but most of my work trips are now to China. The Chinese like their vodka just as much as the Russians. How do you like the United States?"

His openness calmed me. "United States is great. It gave me the opportunity to be what I want, a *Tour Director*. Iran is a nice place too. I read a lot about the country and would love to visit it someday—to meet the people, see the culture and try local foods."

"Definitely come, Iran has a lot to offer. But when you visit, use the Russian passport, not the American. Iran, Russia and China are good friends. There are problems with Americans right now. If you come as a Russian, you'll have no problem at all. As an American, it may be dangerous. At least for now. Iran is next to Turkey, and dangerous people come from there," he said with a serious face.

"That's interesting. I didn't realize there was so much trouble between the United States and Iran. That's too bad. There's so much history in Iran. I'd like to study it and visit the sights."

"There is definitely a lot of history in Iran. Did you know that chess was created in Iran? Although, it was Persia at the time. Iran is also one of the oldest civilizations in the world and we are amazing poets. There is poetry in everything we do. Poetry tells our history. It expresses our feelings and people cite poetry in their daily lives."

His story enlightened me. "I did not realize this. How fascinating. I love poetry and read it in my free time. I'll have to look up the poetry in Iran. Thank you for sharing. As for chess, I've played it since I was a child. My grandfather taught me. I'm actually a ranked chess player in the United States and proud of it. By the way, my name is Aleksey. What's your name?"

"My name is Ebrahim. It's nice to meet you." We shook hands.

"It's nice to meet you too. Please tell me more about the history of Iran." For the next hour, we talked about Iran, China and his work.

When Ebrahim left for his flight, I replaced the backpack in front of me. With my legs on top, I slowly drifted to sleep.

Chapter 4

The plastic chair hurt my back. I tossed and turned but couldn't find the right spot. Loud routine safety announcements jolted me awake every thirty minutes. I couldn't take the noise anymore and put ear buds in and listened to music.

Only after fatigue set in and my eyelids felt heavy, I drifted into the land of darkness. I awoke every so often, mesmerized by the unusual dreams I'd dreamed. One was about China being overrun by zombies. While another involved a vivid aerial battle with guns blazing and planes crashing into the ocean. As scary as the dreams were, the thrill of experiencing them excited me.

I recalled reading that a person could only remember the last dream they'd dreamt before waking. If woken up several times during the night, multiple dreams could be remembered. This night I recalled a whole TV series of dreams.

In the morning, I felt groggy and wished I'd had a comfortable bed. I got up from the seat, picked up my backpack and went to check in for the flight. Domestic flight paperwork and the security check took less than ten minutes. My next flight would take me to Chengdu, where I'd spend the night at a hostel, then fly to Kathmandu, Nepal, the next day.

I boarded the airplane and noticed it to be mostly empty. I sat down, continued listening to music and wrote the daily events in my journal. The act of writing served as both a record and a type of personal meditation.

As I scribbled away, I felt the airplane taking off. The engine kicked in and my body pressed hard against the seat. It had finally become more comfortable. I stopped writing and looked out the window.

Shanghai fascinated me. I saw the endless expanse of the city and a large number of fishing boats along the coastline. As we flew farther, fields of farmland dominated the land, evenly partitioned into squares. This meticulous land organization earned my respect, but at the same time, conflicting emotions arose.

The land below had lost its wilderness. It now looked perfectly tame and tailored to fit the inhabitants' lifestyle. Like an open box with a gift inside, although just as valuable, the thrill of the surprise was gone.

The world has been explored and mapped. Cultures were losing their individuality. The way of the modern world enticed cultures to conform to the boring, yet profitable, lifestyle of the same. Was I selfish to ask for impoverished individuality instead of a unified world of indistinguishability?

There were fewer and fewer remote destinations to explore. A world filled with popular business chains, and experiencing exotic cultures from within the comforts of a coach, scared me more than prison. The way of adventure was now something read in a book rather than experienced.

Trying to shake off these gloomy thoughts, I rested my head, closed my eyes and remembered that I had finally started my adventure. China awaited. The feeling of anticipation exhilarated me.

As my lips turned into a smile, I heard a flight attendant trying to get my attention. I opened my eyes, took out my ear buds and listened to her.

"We will be serving breakfast soon. Would you like chicken, or salmon?"

Despite a short three-and-a-half-hour flight, the airline still offered a full meal.

"I'll have the salmon, please."

She noted my order, smiled and went on to ask the next passenger. Glancing around, I seemed to be the only foreigner on the airplane. In a short moment, the attendant returned with a tray of food.

"What would you like to drink?"

"Tea, please."

She poured a cup and walked away. As I took a sip, the rich

taste of warm, green tea overwhelmed my taste buds. Not like an ocean wave violently crashing upon the shore, but more like a gentle stream flowing down a mountain, slowly feeding the land around it.

The tea rejuvenated my senses and refreshed my mind. I noted to ask for its brand later. Then again, it could have simply been the taste of a new adventure.

After finishing my plate of salmon, salad, fruit mix and pasta, I still felt hungry. Flagging down the flight attendant with my hand, I asked for seconds.

I expected the disapproving glare that I normally received in the United States, but the young woman smiled. "Of course. I will bring another plate. Would you like the salmon or chicken?"

"Chicken, please."

She came back with the food and refilled my cup of green tea. After the meal, the flight attendant came over, and asked, "Could you please fill out a comment card for us?"

"Of course. I would be happy to." She handed me the card with an Air China pen, and told me to keep the pen afterward.

The comment card had routine questions, which included the quality of service, staff and cleanliness of the airplane. Her genuine smile inspired me to write a positive comment and give five out of five stars for everything, especially the food. That truly won me over. I still remembered my aunt's wisdom, "The way to a man's heart is through his stomach." During the past few years, I started to believe her.

~*~*~

Upon landing at the *Chengdu Shuangliu International Airport*, I exited the airplane and went in search of the information desk. I needed directions to the hostel.

Past security, I expected to find numerous currency exchangers, stores and information desks, but all I saw were a few closed stores and several taxi drivers in search of victims. The only service of use to me was a lone currency exchange booth.

The exchange rate offered 6.2 *yuan* for one US dollar. It was better than I expected. Usually airports had the most unfavorable exchange rates, and from experience, I knew going to a local bank offered a better exchange.

I needed yuan for the hostel and transportation. I approached the reception window. "*Ne-hao,*" I said hello in Chinese. "Do you speak English?"

She smiled and shook her head. "No, little."

I smiled back. "Exchange money. Dollar to yuan. OK?"

She understood and collected my one-hundred-dollar bill and passport. After she returned the exchanged currency, I took out a paper with a bus number and showed it to her. "Bus, where?"

She looked at it and pointed outside, across the road where all the other buses were. I thanked her and exited the terminal.

Buses came and went like waves on a shore, endlessly. I walked to the closest bus stop outside the airport and regretted not doing the research ahead of time. Although I'd found a complimentary computer at the Shanghai airport and quickly wrote directions to Lazy Bones Hostel, my instructions weren't clear.

When the bus arrived, the driver stepped out. As if by magic, people appeared and crowded around. I stood there, baffled, as my first place in line turned to the twentieth. Young and old Chinese people pushed each other and tossed their luggage next to the driver at an opportune moment. Afterward, they ran into the bus and picked a good seat.

The people disregarded me like a street lamp in the middle of a day. I needed to act now or I'd have to wait for the next bus. With renewed purpose, I took off my backpack and used it as a shield to push through the crowd of people in front of me. I expected complaints and angry glares but got neither.

I approached the bus driver, who picked up the bags and tossed them with great zeal inside the luggage compartment. With the written address in hand, I called out and put the paper in front of his face. "*Ne-hao, Ne-hao.* Your bus go here?"

His face showed surprise as he paused for a moment and

looked at the paper, and then at me.

I pointed at the paper in my hand again. "Bus go here?"

He nodded and pointed at my luggage.

I gave him my green backpack, and asked, "Please tell me when I arrive at my stop. OK?" He nodded again and threw my backpack into the compartment with the others.

Now that I'd found the right bus, I boarded and picked a window seat. I took out my camera and put it in a holster attached to my belt. Photography was one of my hobbies. I believed in taking as many pictures as possible, and then picking out my favorite after the trips.

As the bus made its way through the city, I took in the view. The scenery looked different than I imagined. It reminded me of a large Chinatown back home.

The cars were small but numerous. Motorbikes swarmed every available part of the road, like flies on a pile of dung. Cars honked them away, but the small, maneuverable motorbikes refilled the empty spaces again and again. I took out my camera and photographed the mayhem in action.

After an hour, I worried. Several people disembarked, but the driver hadn't signaled me. The bus made another stop. The driver yelled out a few words in Chinese and went outside. Everyone got up, picked up their luggage and started to leave. I did the same.

I stepped out and watched the driver unload all the bags.

When the crowd thinned, I picked up my backpack and approached him. "*Ne-hao.* Is this my stop?" I pointed at the paper in my hand.

He quickly glanced at me and nodded. With a quick pace, he went into the bus, closed the door and drove away. There I stood, in the middle of a street corner, with people selling vegetables and fish all around me—the paper still in my hand.

What just happened? I couldn't figure it out. Was I at the right place, or had the driver jilted me? "Oh well." I said aloud, then took in a deep breath of exhaust-filled air and smiled. May the adventure begin.

I looked around and saw a residential, outdoor food market, with crowds of people making bargains. I smelled fish, saw different vegetables for sale and observed small stands selling street food. Some dishes I knew, others I didn't. I doubted anyone spoke English.

I put on my oversized, green backpack and walked toward the main street in the direction where the bus had come from. After turning at the corner of a multi-story building, I noticed business offices on the entire first floor.

I approached the closest office, one with a Travel Agency sign displayed in English, and walked inside. A man sitting behind the desk didn't speak English but pointed to an office next door.

I walked into the referred office and saw a woman standing behind a counter. She noticed me and said a few words in Chinese.

"*Ne-hao*" I replied with a smile. "English?"

"No, no," she responded, and then asked a question I did not understand.

I was about to give up and leave, when a man standing nearby spoke up. "I speak English. Can I help you with anything?" he asked.

"Great. Thank you. I'm trying to get directions to my hostel. Do you know where this is?" I showed him a paper with the address written in English.

"I am not familiar with this street, but there is a telephone number here. Let me call and ask."

"Thank you."

He took out a *smartphone* and dialed the number. After a few rings, a person answered and they talked in Chinese. He asked for my first name, and then finished the telephone conversation.

"OK, you are in a different part of the city. To get to this address, you need to take a subway that's across the street. Here is the address and the name of your hostel written in Chinese." He handed me a piece of paper. "You should take a taxi. It'll be easier."

"Again, thank you so much for your help. How much do I owe you for the telephone call?"

"No, it's OK. I am happy to help. Where are you from?"

We shared a few more words, and then I left to find the train station. After I walked around the corner and made two more circles around the block, I lost my way. I finally gave up and decided to take a taxi.

Back on the main road, taxis were everywhere. I raised my hand and hoped it would work. Not even a minute passed before a yellow and green car with a taxi sign on top pulled over. I sighed with relief. Some signals were universal no matter the location. The taxi driver said something in Chinese, and I handed him the paper with the address.

"*Do Sha Tien?*" I asked him for the price in Chinese.

He pointed to the meter. I took out a pen, a piece of paper and gestured for him to write down the amount. The driver wrote down the number ten. I nodded my head in agreement and got in, pleasantly surprised that the drive would cost less than a dollar and a half.

Fifteen minutes passed and he dropped me off near the hostel. I clearly saw the Lazy Bones Hostel logo on the other side of the street. I thanked the driver and gave him the ten yuan with five extra as a tip. He smiled, nodded his head and pointed to the hostel.

I crossed the street and walked inside.

A young Chinese woman at the desk greeted me. "Hello and welcome. You must be Alex. A man called earlier and asked for directions, which must have been for you."

After I filled out the necessary check-in paperwork, she highlighted the nearby restaurants, banks and attractions on a map. She also wrote down the hostels complimentary Wi-Fi password, breakfast and dinner prices. Afterward, she escorted me to a room and assigned a bunk bed.

My room had six bunks. All were occupied for the night. I thanked the receptionist, put my backpack in a locker and went outside to find a bank.

As I walked at a steady pace, I marveled at the busy city. Countless numbers of people filled all corners of the streets going about their daily activities. In between the tall buildings, I saw men and women cooking food with woks.

They tossed fried rice with vegetables into the air with a fluid, circular motion, and then replaced the wok on the fire, occasionally sprinkling different spices. I stood watching for several minutes and appreciated their skill. I loved cooking and eating even more.

I continued and lost myself in the flow of the city and even forgot the purpose of this walk. I expected an endless number of bicycles, as seen in documentaries and *National Geographic* magazines, but I was wrong. Their time was gone, now replaced by the more advanced alternative, the motorbike. Endless numbers of them filled the roads and took every available route.

After fifteen minutes of walking, I saw a Bank of China on the corner of a street. The large building took up half a block, with enormous, cascading stairs leading to the main entrance.

As I walked up the stairs to the main entrance, one of several men standing nearby approached me. He said in a low voice, "Change money? I give good price."

I thought about it for a moment and sized-up the middle-aged man. "Twenty American dollar. How much?"

The man looked confused for a moment and pulled out a small calculator. "How many dollars?" He pointed and passed the calculator to me. I typed in the amount and passed it back. The man looked disappointed, typed in an amount of Chinese currency I'd be getting back and showed it to me.

After nodding my head in agreement, he led me inside the bank to the ATM and motioned to wait. He withdrew the agreed amount, handed me the money and went outside to look for more opportunities.

The cultural differences intimated me, and the busy city, with its sheer number of people, tired me out. I decided to go back to the hostel and eat dinner there.

When I came back, I sat down at the bar and ordered an overpriced meal with a beer. Lazy Bones Hostel felt like a homey place. It had a decorated reception desk, an indoor lounge area with a bar, pool table and an outside lounge with a Ping-Pong table.

I ordered another bottle of beer, got up and approached the billiards table.

"Can I play next?" I asked the two people playing.

A young Chinese woman hit the ball into a corner pocket. "Sure, we are almost done."

While watching the game, I remembered a job from my youth working at Wal-Mart, a large supercenter. After saving enough money, I bought my own pool table at the twenty percent employee discount. Afterward, I practiced often and reached a level of proficiency.

I watched her hit the number eight ball in to a side pocket, and then look at me. "You are next."

I broke the rack, heard the familiar sound and enjoyed the moment. After two more turns, she hit the number eight ball into a pocket and concluded the game. I took a second sip of my beer, in silence, and shook my head. "Thank you for the game." I smiled and walked toward the bar.

"You are next," I heard her say behind me to another victim.

Sitting down at the bar, I pulled out a notepad and started pronouncing essential Chinese words.

After a few minutes, the bartender couldn't take listening to my poor pronunciations and intervened. "You are saying this wrong. Let me help you." He smiled every time I said a word in Chinese, and then corrected me and explained that my pronunciation of "How much?" would never be understood.

Soon after, a blond-haired, young man approached and joined us. "He is correct in teaching you how to say 'How much?', at least in this region of China. He is using the local *dialect*. Although you might be understood here, when you go to a different province of China, people there won't understand you."

The bartender didn't seem to mind the interruption and listened to the young man as well.

"There are twenty-three provinces in China, and many of them have their own dialect, each with a different accent. It will be too confusing for you to learn all of them. I recommend that you learn standard *Mandarin*. It's a generally accepted form of the Chinese language, which is understood in all provinces."

I looked at him thoughtfully. "This makes sense. I didn't realize that provinces had their own dialects. I guess it's like accents in different states in the USA. Thanks for explaining that."

"Yeah, no problem. I've lived in China for over half a year now to study Mandarin. It took me a whole week just to figure this out. The most difficult part is the tones and I think that's your problem. Mandarin is a tonal language. You must enunciate the words correctly, or you might end up in an awkward situation." He smiled as if remembering an embarrassing moment.

"Think of Mandarin as a song, having to hit different tones in the same word for it to come out just right. Doesn't this sound like fun?" The young man looked at me grinning.

I laughed. "I think I'll need a few minutes to digest this. I didn't realize it was so complicated. My name is Aleksey by the way. What's yours?"

"I'm Sam. Where do you live in the U.S.?"

"In Florida now, but I used to live in New York City for about seven years. Now I'm on vacation, getting away for a while. You from the States too?"

"Yep, I live in Chicago. I came to China for a year to learn the language. Mandarin speaking jobs are in high demand all over the world now, so here I am. I started in Beijing for a few months, and then decided to see the country and just talk to people. I hire tutors sometimes but am mostly self-taught." Sam looked proud.

"That's great. You know a lot. Big thanks for the explanation and helping me out. How do I pronounce this correctly?" I pointed at a sentence in my notepad.

Sam and I talked for an hour about the language, life and our experiences in China as I bought us beers. In the end, I thanked him again, and we went to play Ping-Pong with a couple from Holland.

After making a few more friends, I ate dinner at the bar and started preparing for tomorrow's trip to the airport. I asked the receptionist for directions and had her write it down on paper in Mandarin. Back at the room, I met my roommates, repacked my backpack and went to sleep.

Part 2

Nepal: To Climb Mount Everest

Chapter 5

A new day had begun. Adventures awaited. After breakfast, I boarded a bus until I reached the airport. There I went through security and eventually boarded the airplane for Kathmandu, Nepal.

The flight time was only three hours, yet Air China still served a full-course meal. As always, I asked for seconds. From experience, a few extra pounds helped slow down the weight loss on these arduous expeditions.

Gaining weight had always been a difficult task for me. In fact, it was impossible. I'd eaten sticks of butter yet it yielded no success. So, when free food presented itself, I accepted without hesitation.

In addition to eating, I'd mastered the art of energy conservation. I tried to be like a lazy street dog that lay in the same spot and didn't waste energy on useless actions or exaggerated movements—only acted when necessary.

I'd honed this skill over the years, because on the road, I never knew when I'd have my next full meal. Excessive actions led to wasted calories and depleted my limited supply of energy.

As the airplane descended over Kathmandu, the chaotic scene below intimidated me. The unsystematic building placement confused me. Yet, at the same time, I found it charming. I felt freedom in this chaos. The people below built their houses wherever they could.

The dark clouds above the city reminded me of fog. Only after several minutes did I realize it was smog. My preexisting idea of a beautiful, clean and nature-friendly Nepal was shattered as I continued staring out the window.

When the airplane touched down, I packed my carry-on bag and prepared to exit onto a ramp and into the terminal. The hatch opened and a ladder conveniently guided me down onto the hard pavement. The scorching sun welcomed me.

After several minutes, a shuttle arrived. As I waited to board, I saw my checked backpack being tossed onto a trailer attached to a tractor. Relief washed over me, but a feeling of worry soon replaced it. Would it make it to the terminal in one piece? The airport looked more like a run-down village than a transportation hub.

The shuttle arrived at the terminal, and I followed the signs to customs. A long, slow-moving line awaited me. The sheer number of people looked more like a horde of insects than a line. Like me, most visitors didn't have a visa to enter Nepal and planned to register for one upon arrival.

I filled out the form and took out a passport photograph for my visa. Alternatively, a photo booth stood conveniently in a corner.

When my turn came, the man at the window took the documents and quickly completed the form. He asked me for forty US dollars, which covered all expenses for a thirty-day visa. He never looked at me, not once. He only focused on the papers and the computer.

After finalizing the form, he passed it to me without giving me a glance, and then called for the next person. Despite his lack of attention, I appreciated the simplicity of indifference.

~*~*~

Afterward, I collected my luggage and proceeded toward an information desk. While waiting in line, I worried about finding a hotel for the night. I had not researched Kathmandu and was clueless about the city. While deep in thought, a man behind me tapped my shoulder.

"Excuse me. Do you have a pen I can use?"

The sudden motion startled me, but I quickly regained my composure. "Ah . . . yes, let me check." I handed over the pen. He wore a casual, grey business suit, no tie and a white shirt with the top button undone. Middle aged, with graying black hair, he had an air of composure about him.

After filling out the form, he handed back the pen. "Here,

thank you."

I smiled. "No problem. Are you in Nepal for the first time?"

"No, I am often here for business. I need to fax some paperwork before I leave the airport. What about you?"

"Yeah, I just flew in. I'm trying to figure out where to stay for the night at a reasonable price and a good location. Do you have any recommendations?"

"Definitely, I love this city. I've been here many times and considered moving here sometime in the future. Since it's your first time, I recommend you go to the old town of Kathmandu. It's called Thamel. Most backpackers go there, and it's *the* place to see in the city.

"You'll find old temples, historic sites, outdoor markets and much more. Although the old town offers many *guesthouses*, I recommend the Thamel Grand Hotel to start with. It's not expensive. The room prices vary from thirty to fifty dollars per night, which includes the necessary amenities of a standard American hotel. It's easy to find. Any taxi will know where it is. That's where I stayed during my backpacking days and highly recommend it. Everything you need is within walking distance."

"Thank you for the information. I didn't prepare well enough and your recommendation is greatly appreciated. It's good to meet an experienced traveler."

As the line progressed, we talked about his backpacking days and the city of Kathmandu. When our turn came, we said goodbye and I proceeded to the information desk.

"Welcome. What can I help you with?" a bleary-eyed, sulking Nepalese woman asked.

"Hi, I'm looking for a place to stay for the night. Could you recommend something inexpensive in Thamel?"

"There are many options. Here is a list. Do you have other questions?" She looked impatient as she handed me the paper.

"Yes. If I wanted to get to the Thamel Grand Hotel, is there a local bus available, and how much would it cost?"

"City busses can be found outside, but I recommend you

take a taxi. The bus price is ten *rupees*. A prepaid taxi will take you to the hotel for seven hundred and fifty rupees. Take the taxi. There might not be enough space on the bus for your luggage." She pointed to my large, dark-green backpack.

After declining the taxi, I thanked her for the information and walked outside to consider my options. I calculated the exchange rate to be eighty-four rupees for each dollar.

~*~*~

As I contemplated whether to take a bus or a taxi, the chaotic surroundings brought me back to reality. Lines of people amassed everywhere. Piles of garbage were scattered in all corners, and small, rusty taxis filled the nearby parking lot. Before I could move farther, several people raced toward me.

"America? France? Russia? I know a good man to give you cheap price for *trek* in mountains. Come this way," a dark-skinned man said in English and pulled at my arm.

"Wait! You need taxi to Thamel? I give cheap price, only five hundred rupees or six US dollars," another man said.

I stood silent for a moment and decided to give the first man a counter offer.

Before I said a word, the second man saw my hesitation. "No problem, four hundred and fifty rupees. For you my friend, only the best price. My taxi is there, come."

"Cheap taxi, cheap tour to mountains, come with me," another stranger called out behind me.

"Don't pull him. I saw him first!" several others joined in.

Before I realized it, a dozen men surrounded me and shouted out different services. I felt overwhelmed and didn't know what to do. I wanted a minute of silence to gather my thoughts and start again, but that seemed impossible.

"I want a taxi to Thamel. One hundred rupees. You?" I pointed to one of them.

He shook his head. "No, no, that's too little. Five hundred rupees."

"One hundred rupees to Thamel. Anyone?" I yelled out.

"That's too little. Five hundred, OK?" another said.

I knew my price was too low but didn't care. I just needed a reason to leave. After receiving several counter offers, I declined them all and walked away.

As I started to run, they followed without losing a step and kept shouting questions. One of them blocked my path, and asked, "Where are you from?"

"Russia," I said slowing down.

"We love Russians. Come this way. We have a Russian translator just over there. Come with us." The man pointed to a car a hundred feet away and pulled my arm to follow him.

I didn't know what to do and simply followed, shocked that they had a translator in the parking lot. I noticed the men who surrounded me no longer fought among each other. They seemed to have made a silent agreement of cooperation to get my business. One of them ran on ahead and talked to the translator.

As I tried to think of how to get away, we stopped. A tall man stood in front and looked at me as if I were a bag of gold coins.

"You are Russian? We have many Russians here. What are you looking for? A taxi? A cheap guided mountain tour?" He spoke Russian fluently and kept rambling on with his questions.

After he listed his services, they all looked at me in silence and waited for an answer. They had put me on the spot, and I felt pressured by their stares.

"Where is the bus?" I asked with an anxious look on my face.

"The bus is ten minutes away, but don't take it. There will be too many people. Your big backpack won't fit inside and will need to be placed on top. Take a taxi. It's safer. I know a good hotel for a cheap price in Thamel. I can take you there. Here is my taxi. Let's go."

"No, thank you." I was fed up with all the people around me and no longer cared about being polite. I pushed my way through the crowd to get away. I was angry, tired and felt somewhat helpless.

As I left them, the first man who'd offered me a taxi approached.

"OK, OK. I take you to Thamel for three hundred rupees. I know a good hotel there." He must have seen the defensive look on my face, and added, "Don't worry. We take care of you. Nepalese people are good. We want you to be happy."

I wasn't sure whether it was the sincere look on the man's face or my mental fatigue that made me accept. "Three hundred rupees to Thamel. Let's go," I said.

The man motioned for me to follow. In a moment we arrived at a small car so rusty, I was unable to discern its model.

"Sit in the back," he said, then opened the door for me. He sat in the front passenger seat. After a few words to the driver, the car started to move. The back seats were so small they barely fit both my backpack and me.

"I take you to a good hotel in Thamel. Many backpackers stay there. If you want trekking to Mount Everest, or Pokhara, they help you at the front desk. Nepal is a beautiful country. You will like it here and want to come back in the future." He smiled and turned around to face the road.

I finally relaxed, leaned back and took in the view. As we drove out of the airport, I tried to understand the mayhem around me. There were too many people, and no one obeyed the traffic signs. Animals pulled carts across the road carelessly, motorbikes flooded the streets, and everyone honked and tried to rush ahead.

After fifteen minutes, our car left the main road and turned onto a small, unpaved street. I looked around, overwhelmed, and gripped the door handle as we drove over the potholes.

Buildings of all sizes surrounded me. It looked as if a bomb had fallen and destroyed the walls, roofs and scattered rubble everywhere. The people within the buildings were the only comforting sight.

In one house, with missing walls, I saw a family sitting around a small fire cooking food. In another, I heard a group of people yelling at each other. No one backed down.

As we made another turn, the car stopped. A cow had blocked the road. The driver honked several times without any sign of anger on his face, as if it were just another normal day at work. I was surprised to see that the cow never bothered to turn around to look at the honking car.

While the driver waited for the cow to leave, a skinny, old man caught my attention. He lay close to a house, on the side of the road, dressed in dirty, tattered clothing with hordes of flies surrounding him. I didn't understand what was happening at first, but after seeing his blank, lifeless eyes, I realized he was dying. It didn't take a doctor to figure it out. A man lay dying, in the middle of a street, as others walked past him with indifference.

I opened my mouth and tried to say something, but no words came out. As the car started to move, panic set in. What was I doing in Nepal for a whole month? I didn't want to be here a second longer. Where was the driver taking me?

As these questions flooded my mind, one stood out from the rest. Was my driver taking me to some remote house where I'd be attacked and robbed? This thought started to take root, and my imagination ran wild with other similar scenarios. I took a deep breath. I had to keep it together. Panic would not help the situation.

I calmed down and remembered past trips to exotic locations around the world. During my first days, I often felt helpless and weary, but people's kindness proved me wrong every time.

My previous travels reminded me that people are generally good and should be given a chance. I needed to give myself a full day before I judged others and made serious decisions. At the moment, I needed to find a place for the night.

"To which hotel are we going?" I asked.

The man must have noticed the panic in my voice. "It's located in the center of Thamel. They speak English and will help answer questions. Other foreigners stay there too. Why do you come to Nepal?" He took out a cigarette, put it in his mouth and offered me one.

I declined with a smile. "I want to go to Mount Everest and see how far I can climb. Do you know where I can buy maps and find transportation to the mountain?"

"We arrive soon. I tell hotel and they find you a person to help." For the next fifteen minutes, he explained minor details of the trek.

The car stopped outside the gates of a clean, orange-colored, four-story building.

"We are here. Let's go inside and get you a room."

I stepped out of the taxi and walked through the gates. A grassy courtyard, with tables and chairs, greeted me. Foreigners of all ages sat comfortably as they ate and conversed.

They reminded of old, English men sitting at tables, smoking cigars and sipping whiskey as they talked about their adventures around the world. Several Nepalese women served them. I followed my unofficial guide to the front desk.

My driver spoke to a man in Nepali, and then introduced him to me. "This is Bishal. He owns this hotel and will help you. Check in first. When done, remember to pay me. I wait outside."

I nodded to the driver, and then faced Bishal. "Hi. How much for one night?"

"Hello, and welcome to our hotel. We are located at the center of Thamel, and everything you need is nearby. Stores, restaurants and many attractions are a few minutes away. Your room has a clean, king-size bed, your own bathroom, air-conditioning, free *Wi-Fi*, and there is a receptionist at the desk twenty-four hours a day. Our price is very cheap, only forty US dollars."

I knew it was too much but didn't have the energy to argue or look elsewhere. "OK, I'll stay for the night. I also need help finding a map and transportation."

"Yes, we already have Paul on his way here to help you with everything. I need to make a copy of your passport and collect the forty US dollars."

I paid for the hotel and Bishal led me to the room.

"This is your key. You can leave your items inside, no one will take them. When you are ready, go downstairs. Remember to pay your driver. Paul will be waiting for you at the desk in a few minutes."

"Thank you, I will be down soon." I stepped inside, closed the door and let out a sigh. After placing the backpack in a corner, I sat on the bed and enjoyed a moment of peace. Several minutes later, I took out a smaller backpack, placed my valuables inside, locked the door and went downstairs.

~*~*~

At the desk, a short, middle-aged Nepalese man greeted me. "Hello, and welcome to Nepal. My name is Paul. I will help you with everything you need and answer all of your questions. When you are ready, please follow me to my office just a few blocks away on foot." He had a pleasant smile and a trustworthy look about him.

"Sounds good. Let me pay the driver, and then we can go."

I stepped outside and found the driver. "Thank you for bringing me here. This is four hundred and fifty rupees. I gave you a little extra for the help."

"Thank you, and enjoy Nepal," he said as he walked back to the taxi.

I returned to the hotel. "Paul, I'm ready."

"OK, please follow me. My office is fifteen minutes away. We are going to take a left as we exit and walk to the plaza ahead. I will also bring you back to the hotel, but if you wish to go back on your own, pay attention to the surroundings."

As we walked, Paul answered several questions and told me a bit about the city. I had a good impression of this professional, courteous man.

The streets split off in many directions and eventually led to various small bazaars. I could not find any street signs. Every street looked similar and made navigation a challenge.

The locals filled the roads selling various trinkets. There were little *shrines* at every corner and foreigners who walked in all directions. I tried to remember the landmarks. After years of experience and getting lost on previous adventures, finding my way now seemed easier.

"My travel agency is in this building, upstairs." Paul said as he pointed to a three-story structure with a large travel agency sign at the top.

We walked up to the third floor and into an office. It had a professional, clean look, a desk in the center, file cabinets on one side and travel posters on the walls.

"Have a seat." He motioned to a chair in front of the desk and sat facing me.

A man brought me a hot cup of tea, and then sat on a chair at the opposite side of the office.

Paul continued, "I've been told you wish to do the *Everest Base Camp* trek. Is that correct?"

"Sounds right, although I'm not familiar with the routes or my options. If all goes well, I might wish to go beyond the Base Camp. I have the necessary equipment and basic climbing experience. Could you please tell me the options?"

Paul took out a map from one of the drawers. "My travel agency offers two Everest Base Camp treks. I will explain them in detail on this map. However, we do not offer Everest *summit* climbing services, and this is not the right season for it."

The answer didn't surprise me, but I wanted to confirm the details. "When is the right season for the summit climb, and how much does it cost?"

"May is the best month because of optimal weather conditions. The start of the climb will depend on the weather. As for the cost, it will be between thirty thousand to forty-five thousand US dollars. This includes the fixed climbing permit price of eleven thousand, the guide fee and other miscellaneous expenses."

I laughed. "This is way more expensive than I expected. I can't believe that the permit is so costly. I guess it makes sense though, to cover the expense of evacuations and emergency procedures. I'm not familiar with the possible routes to get to the Base Camp. Could you show me the most popular one?"

"The two most common routes depend on the time you have available. The shorter option is a sixteen-day round-trip, which starts in the village of Lukla. An airplane will take you there and back. The second option is a twenty-four-day round-trip. You'll need to take a bus from Kathmandu to a town called Jiri, and then walk to Lukla. If you have the time, I recommend the twenty-four-day option. It will help you acclimatize to the altitude and prepare you physically for the more difficult passes ahead. Which one are you interested in?"

"I need to be back in Kathmandu by November 27th for my flight out of Nepal. Could you help me make a bus reservation to the town of Jiri and a flight back to Kathmandu on November 25th from Lukla? And how much will this cost?"

"We can arrange transportation for you, including a guide who will meet you in Jiri and take you to the Everest Base Camp. The price for the twenty-four-day trek will also include all accommodations, dinners and breakfasts. Permit fees are also included. The price for the twenty-four-day excursion is one thousand four hundred US dollars. We accept all major credit cards." Paul smiled.

I thought about his offer, but I did not intend to take a guide. For better or worse, this adventure I wanted to do on my own. Even if I didn't make it halfway, I had to try. I explained so to Paul. He was surprised and tried to dissuade me from going alone, listing the possible dangers of the climb and *altitude sickness*, which can happen at any time.

The man who brought me tea earlier intervened and claimed I wasn't allowed to climb the mountain alone, even to the Base Camp. Paul gave him a stern look, and the man didn't interrupt again.

I persisted with my decision and declined Paul's offer of a cheaper price or help finding a travel companion. In the end, Paul seemed to understand he could not convince me and marked the map with all possible accommodations before the Base Camp.

He explained the dangerous passes and locations where I'd need to use *crampons* for stability to walk on *glaciers*. Then he arranged a trekking permit and reserved both the bus leaving tomorrow for Jiri and the airplane back.

In the end, I realized that Paul was not only a businessman but also a good person. He seemed genuinely worried about my well-being and charged a small amount for his services.

After the briefing and paperwork, I gave Paul a generous tip because I believed his kindness needed to be recognized, and money shows that best. Paul encouraged me to visit him again before I left Nepal. As I walked out of the office and into the streets, I no longer felt distraught. I now had a passionate desire to start the climb.

~*~*~

Glancing at the winding roads, I felt confident I'd find my way back to the hotel. The evening approached, and I didn't want to return until I ate. On the way to the travel agency, I'd noticed a local restaurant that occupied the main floor of a three-story building with many foreigners eating inside. A sign at the top advertised The Yak Restaurant.

When I walked in, I saw a large, decorated room with square tables in corners and an open center. A young host greeted me, led me to a table, and then handed me a menu. It showed pictures for most options, with descriptions below in English. The ample, unique selections appealed to me.

In the end, I picked the yak sizzler steak with rice and veggies on the side. I remembered *yak* being in the same family as cattle. They were similar in most traits except that yak grunt, whereas cattle moo. Yak also have longer hair.

After a short wait, a server placed a large portion of food in front of me. A fragrant, sizzling steak sat atop cast iron with a wooden board underneath. It made my mouth salivate. Several people turned with curiosity as the aroma of the meat permeated the room. The steak tasted like beef but tougher.

After finishing my meal, I felt unsure about tipping. Looking around for assistance, I saw a couple sitting behind me who were speaking Russian. "Excuse me. Do you know if tipping is customary in Nepal?"

The man replied, "Now that's a surprise. I didn't expect you to speak Russian. Why are you sitting all alone? Come, move over and join us. I'll tell you about tipping while we share a drink."

Pleasantly surprised by his friendliness, I accepted the offer and sat with them. The man had dark-brown hair and looked to be in his mid-forties. The woman had blond, shoulder-length hair and seemed to be a few years younger.

"I'm surprised to see Russians here too. My name is Aleksey."

"I am Dimitri." We shook hands.

"Hello, my name is Elizabeth. I am happy you joined us. What are your plans in Nepal?"

"I'm here to do the Everest climb. I arrived today and still getting used to the culture. Everything is much different from what I expected, but I'm slowly adjusting." I sighed.

"Stay strong. I am sure you are doing great. Dimitri and I are also starting the Everest climb in a few days. There are seven people in our group, and we will meet the rest of our party tomorrow. Where are you from?" Elizabeth asked.

Before I could speak another word, Dimitri interrupted, and said, "Hold that thought. Before we continue, a toast to our meeting is in order. Finish the water in your glass."

He quickly looked around and stealthily reached for a bag under the table, then picked it up and pulled out a large bottle of vodka. Taking our empty glasses, he poured a generous amount. After placing the bottle back in the bag, he raised his glass. "To making new friends and reuniting with others."

I raised my drink, gulped down half of it and embraced the stereotype of Russians' love for vodka. When my Russian origin came up in a conversation, the topic of vodka was commonly discussed. From my experience, most believe Russians to be vodka-swilling fanatics, which is not far from the truth. I just happen to be an exception.

"Thank you for the drink. I live in the United States and can't wait to do the Everest climb."

Dimitri bit off a piece of a pickle. "Elizabeth and I are also looking forward to the climb. This trip is a reunion for us. It's been seven years since the last time we saw each other. I moved to Israel and Elizabeth stayed in Moscow. Meeting in Nepal to climb the mountain is a great way for us to reunite and spend time together."

She looked at Dimitri with a gentle smile. "It's been so long since we've seen each other. Wasn't our last meeting by the lake outside Moscow?"

"Yes, I remember that day. We spent half the day jumping off a rock into the water. In the evening, we made a fire and watched the stars. It was a great day. I felt sad leaving for Israel soon after. You should have answered my letters sooner." Dimitri glanced at Elizabeth with a sad expression, but quickly recovered. "Let me refill our glasses so we can have another toast. To new adventures and a safe journey ahead of us."

"I'll drink to that." I prepared my glass for a refill.

For the next half hour, we talked about Russia, the upcoming climb and the unique culture of Nepal. Dimitri also explained the customs of tipping in Nepal and its importance to help support the local economy.

The sun had set and the bottle of vodka reached its end. As the three of us were enjoying each other's company, Dimitri looked at me. "I want to thank you for joining us. When you sat at our table, we had reunited a few minutes prior. I wasn't sure what to say to my beautiful Elizabeth. With you here, I was able to open up. Thank you for that."

Elizabeth nodded. "I agree with Dimitri. Thank you, Aleksey. Before we leave, let's take a picture together." After the photograph, we shared our emails and parted ways.

On the way back, I staggered a little but managed to purchase food and water for tomorrow's long bus drive. At the hotel, I reserved a taxi to the bus station, and then went up the stairs to my room. Bishal, the owner of the hotel, had not lied. My backpack, with all its contents, remained intact in the corner of the room where I had left it.

I showered, shaved, organized and went to sleep early. My last thoughts were of Nepal and that one month here would not be enough. There was so much to see, yet so little time.

Chapter 6

Jet lag caused me to toss and turn the whole night. I gave up trying to fall asleep and took advantage of the free Wi-Fi to check my email. The news of my friend's upcoming, arranged marriage surprised me. Despite the interesting situation leading to it, he appeared to enjoy the occasion. I replied with congratulations, and then started packing.

Before sunrise, I stood bleary eyed outside the hotel and waited for the taxi. It arrived on time, and I sat in the front and looked at the darkened streets. I found it interesting to see the usually busy roads, now empty, with the exception of an occasional shop owner sweeping. It seemed as though they collected the trash into piles and moved it across the road. Who knows? Maybe they didn't like their neighbors.

The driver honored his promise and made it to the bus station within fifteen minutes. I paid him a little extra and exited the taxi. After crossing the street, I saw an unpaved field with buses and large vehicles parked next to each other. There were people with bags waiting in lines. Conductors yelled out bus routes and locals sold food to travelers.

In Nepal, conductors worked with the bus drivers to collect money and answered questions. On longer routes, two drivers took shifts and alternated between driving and conducting. There were no coin dispensers or computers to process the payments as passengers came and went en masse.

The loud noises of the bus station hurt my ears, but it helped me to stay focused. I had to find my bus and couldn't repeat the mistake I'd made in China where I was jilted.

The nearest conductor shouted bus numbers confidently and seemed like the right person to ask for directions. I approached and pointed to a number on my ticket. "Excuse me. Where is this bus?"

He looked at my ticket. "Follow me." After we passed several vehicles, he pointed. "Your bus."

"Thank you." I walked inside and confirmed my destination with the driver. He took my luggage and showed me my seat. The standard twenty-four-seat *Tata* bus offered little legroom. I sat down and hoped the bus wouldn't fill up.

My hopes were short-lived as two men walked toward me to occupy the last available seats. The older of the two approached and bowed. He then smiled and pointed at the empty seat next to me. I quickly got up and let him sit by the window. The other man sat in empty seat across the aisle.

When the bus moved, I looked over to my seatmate. He wore a reddish-orange robe and held *Tibetan prayer beads*. He looked exactly like a Tibetan monk from the movies I'd seen.

The sun rose as we drove out of the city. The orange colors glistened and enveloped the buildings outside the window. Despite the gentle warmth of the sun, the bumpy ride, with its sharp twists and turns, prevented me doing anything other than listening to music and admiring the views.

For the first few hours, the bus followed a highway that changed to a smaller, two-lane road. I couldn't even call it a road because there were no lanes, just a dirt trail passing through mountains.

Whenever a car approached, one of the two vehicles made a complete stop to let the other pass or faced the consequences of the unguarded cliff to its side. At first, I held my breath, but then relaxed and simply enjoyed the experience.

There were no bathrooms, and the driver made no stops. Lunch marked our four-hour halfway point and the only break. The small hilltop village by the road offered a panoramic view. I looked at the altimeter on my watch. It showed a surprising three thousand meters. When converted to feet, it was more than triple, over nine thousand.

As I stepped out of the bus to eat with the rest of the passengers, I paused for a moment to take in the scenery. Mount Everest stood far in the distance in all its glory, tall and majestic but not the tallest. Closer mountains appeared taller, and only

Mount Everest's signature peak distinguished it from others. Mount Everest was still a young mountain and grew about four inches each a year.

Across the road, outside a restaurant, people formed a line with plates in their hands, waiting for a woman behind a wooden counter to serve them food. When my turn came, she asked my choice. I pointed to the plate of food a man was eating at a nearby table. I didn't know the language or the local cuisine well enough to make a tasteful selection.

While I ate, a couple nearby chatted in English. I overheard them call my dish *dal bhat.* It consisted of steamed rice, beans and cooked lentil soup called dal, a staple food in Nepal and India. Despite the spiciness, I thoroughly enjoyed it, if not for the taste, then for the large amount given.

After lunch, the driver called everyone back and we continued. In order to make better use of my time, I practiced Nepali with the two monks who spoke English. "This is so much easier than Chinese. Thank you for helping me practice. Where are you two from?"

"We are *Buddhist monks* from Dharamsala, India. Now we are traveling to Jiri. The small village needs our help. We will stay at the local temple for several months before going to the next village. I understand you are also going to Jiri. If you wish, we could recommend a guesthouse. We stayed there before, and a family took good care of us. They have nice rooms and won't take much money from you."

"That'd be wonderful." Their recommendation was welcome because I hadn't planned my stays. The rest of the drive was normal, with the exception of driving over a chicken in a small village. I didn't realize it to be a serious matter until the bus stopped, and everyone got off to witness the scene of the crime. When I stepped out, I saw an older woman yelling at the driver. The poor man had difficulty talking back.

It seemed as though half of the village came to see them argue. I counted almost fifty people. In the end, the driver gave her cash, and the crowd dissipated. Afterward, he picked up the bloody chicken, packed it in a plastic bag and strapped it atop the bus. It would probably serve as his dinner later tonight. All of us got back inside, and the bus drove significantly faster than before. It must have been an expensive chicken.

The skills of the driver amazed me. We drove on dirt roads on mountains with no guardrails. The roads twisted and turned, obstructing the view ahead. Before every turn, the driver honked. If he heard a honk back, from the other side of the bend, he stopped and let the other vehicle pass because of the narrow passage. Otherwise, he kept driving at full speed, oblivious to what awaited him beyond the turn. I lacked the skills and experience to drive in such a chaotic manner and silently admired him.

After nine hours on the road, the people around me started to prepare for their arrival. The bus slowed to a stop and everyone started to get out. I went to get my backpack from a large pile of luggage stacked inside the back of the bus.

When I picked it up, I turned around and saw the two monks exiting. The younger one looked at me but did not motion to follow him. When they left, a crowd of people got inside and advertised their services in English, which mostly included a "cheap hotel." It appeared the monks left the decision to me. Immediately, I refused all offers for accommodation and went outside to follow my newly made friends.

The two monks waited for me. I said my goodbyes to the older monk, and then I followed the younger one. As we walked across the paved road, I looked around and admired the beautifully colored houses. The reds, whites and blues appeared almost patriotic. We arrived to one such house, and my companion knocked on the door.

~*~*~

A man stepped out. They talked for a moment in Nepali, and then the monk turned and looked at me, and said, "This man is your host. He will give you a room for the night. We usually stay here, but this time the temple has given us a room. It was nice meeting you. Have a safe journey."

I thanked him and then faced my new host.

"Hello, come inside." The man spoke English well. "Follow me. I'll take you to your room." We walked through a corridor and into a kitchen. "Our family dinner will start at seven. Is that time OK for you?"

"Seven is good."

"OK. Be in the kitchen then. What would you like to eat?"

The only local options I knew of were dal bhat and yak steak. Both seemed good, but I wanted to try something different. "I'll have whatever your family is making tonight. Will that be OK?"

"That's fine. We will eat dal bhat. It's rice, beans and soup."

"I've had it before. Thank you."

We walked out of the kitchen and into a long hallway. There were several wooden doors. Each had unique, decorative carvings, which made them easy to distinguish

He approached one on the left, took out a key and opened it. "This is your room for the night. Here is your key. Please don't lose it. Give it back to me in the morning. The toilet is outside through the door at the end of the hallway. Oh, and I will collect the money tomorrow at breakfast." He handed me the key and walked back to the kitchen.

I stepped inside the small room and noticed two beds with floral-colored blankets. Sunlight illuminated the blue-colored walls and brightened the atmosphere. I placed my backpack next to a bed and started unpacking. With over four hours until dinner, I decided to explore the town and check my route for tomorrow's trek. I locked the door and went outside.

Despite being a small, mountain village, the town of Jiri surprised me with its colors and busy streets. Almost all of the buildings stretched along the main road and only several lonely houses, which included the local temple, stood out in the distance. The abundance of outdoor equipment sold by vendors indicated this to be a popular trekker's destination.

The local businesses included several small restaurants, stores and a local bar, which had the biggest sign in town. The two-story poster showed a muscular, shirtless Nepalese man standing with a woman hugging him from behind. In big, bold letters, it read, *COMMANDO, SUPER STRONG BEER* and pictured a beer bottle on the bottom, right corner.

I wasn't sure if it was my dry throat or the big bold letters on the poster tempting me to try it. I took out a bottle of water and drank it to quench my thirst. Only after, did I go to see the rest of town. What a powerful advertisement.

As I walked, I saw a pattern of two to three-story buildings aligned next to each other and several large trucks on the side of the road unloading supplies. Business signs dominated most of the buildings and advertised hotels, trekking services, equipment and other services in English. I stopped by a small, outdoor food store and bought the necessities for tomorrow's journey.

The town fascinated me at first but slowly grew monotonous. I proceeded to the local temple. It proved easy to find, where a large, white *stupa* stood on the highest hill in town. During my earlier conversation with the monks, they explained that stupa meant dome-shaped structure, erected as a *Buddhist shrine*, which represented a specific aspect of enlightenment.

When I arrived, I saw a group of six young girls playing cards on the grass below the stupa. Card games intrigued me, and I wanted to find out the game they played. Their ages appeared to be between eight and twelve. They didn't pay attention to me at first, but as I got closer, they stopped playing and looked at me. I smiled and waved.

"What are you playing?" I pointed at the cards in their hands. The girls giggled and looked at me shyly.

"We play Dhumbal," said one of the more confident girls. "Want to join?"

She surprised me with her English skills.

"OK. I'll watch you play and learn." I sat down on the grass next to them and tried to understand it but had difficulty grasping the rules. All six of them tried to teach me the game, but only one of them spoke minimal English. I enjoyed watching them play and conversed the best I could.

"You live in this town?" I pointed at the English-speaking girl.

"Yes, my home, there." She pointed to a house next to the main road in the distance. "You from where?"

"America."

My answer caused several "Oh's," and "Ah's," and then more giggles. One of the girls said something in Nepali and pointed at my face.

"My friend say you have nice, white teeth. You look pretty."

"Oh, thank you very much. Tell your friend I have a small gift for her and the rest of you." I opened my backpack, pulled out several caramel candies and gave each girl two. "This is for you, for teaching me to play the card game. Thank you."

They were surprised but took the candies, unwrapped each one and ate them immediately. I played the next round and, with their help, learned the basics. After several games, we took a picture together, and then I went back to the main road to find the trail for tomorrow.

When I reached the end of the village, the paved road turned into a wooded trail. Several locals nearby confirmed this path to be the one I needed.

Afterward, I returned to my room and studied the maps. At seven, I went to the kitchen, saw Aastic, my host, and met his family. His wife served dal bhat to everyone. When I ate the first spoonful of rice and beans covered in sauce, I felt a tear slowly run down my cheek. The food tasted delicious but spicy enough to make my eyes water.

Aastic laughed. "I see you are not used to spicy food. My wife made it less spicy for you, but it must still be too much. Let me get a different plate for you."

"No, this is delicious. Please don't mind my reaction. Thank you for the food." I took a cup of water and drank half of it. "I am happy that you have spicy food for me. I need to start getting used to it."

"Eat the bread. It helps reduce the spicy flavor better than water. I respect your choice and believe it will also help your stomach. The hot spices act as an antibiotic in the digestive tract and prevent diarrhea. It also stimulates appetite in hot, tropical areas and makes you sweat to cool off the body. I feel discouraged that the new generation doesn't know this and simply use spices as a flavor." He sighed and shook his head as if remembering something.

"That is interesting. I didn't realize spices have such benefits. I can confidently say I won't have problems with hunger." I laughed.

As we talked about many subjects to pass the time, I had two more helpings of food.

He stood up from the table and picked up a photograph from one of the kitchen drawers. "Here, take a look at this picture. This is my sister. She lives in New Jersey, in America. Do you know where it is?"

"Yes. New Jersey is next to New York City. I've been there many times."

"Maybe someday I'll be able to visit her again and then see the capital." He stood quietly for a moment, "America . . . it's a very rich country."

I didn't disagree with him. After dinner, I went to my room and wrote about the day in my journal.

Chapter 7

The frigid, night air forced me to get out of bed and acquire a second blanket but not before finding my way to the outhouse. It humbled me to find a hole in the ground, which served as a *squat toilet*. My phone light showed a scenic view of the frozen deposits below. After a refreshing outing, I slid under the blankets and slowly drifted to sleep and dreamed of the exciting day ahead.

The morning sun illuminated the blue walls of my room and reminded me to get up. I brushed my teeth, and then went to the kitchen to check on breakfast. It consisted of garlic soup, vegetable salad and *roti*, the traditional bread of Nepal, which seems to go with every meal in this country.

After an energizing meal, I paid for the night and prepared to leave. Stepping outside, I said my goodbyes to Aastic and his family, who had gathered to see me off.

"Thank you, all, for taking care of me. Aastic, get in touch with me if you come to America. You and your family are always welcome to stay at my home in Florida."

The moment I left Jiri, the trail greeted me with a surreal view of small villages in the distance as I climbed higher. I felt both excited and happy to be exactly where I was, trekking up a lonely mountain in Nepal.

I enjoyed my dream for a whole five minutes, until an aching pain in my legs and shoulders brought me back to reality. I huffed and puffed and thought, why, oh why, didn't I exercise more before starting this trip. Or should I have packed less?

My backpack included all of my winter equipment, climbing equipment, a tent, sleeping bag, inflatable mattress, cooking stove, over three liters of water, enough food to last a week and much more. I really wondered if I had over packed, but then remembered I needed to be tough.

A real man needs to be ready for anything. If an abominable

snowman jumped out of the bushes, I'd be prepared with my miniature, *Swiss Army Knife*, which offered not only a pinky-sized blade but also nail clippers.

The real climb would start in Namche Bazaar, which was seven days away. I wanted to make it in five, maybe even four days. My body however, told me otherwise.

After twenty minutes of trekking uphill, I encountered my first nemesis, an unmarked fork in the trail. I remembered the verse from *Robert Frosts'* poem and took "the one less traveled." Soon after, trees and heavy vegetation surrounded me.

Before being certain I made the correct choice, another fork appeared. This one took decision making to a completely different level. It presented me with three possibilities. The map that Paul had given me only had the general route, not the detailed, topographical information.

Undecided, I stood there for a moment, and then noticed a small, red string tied to the branch of a tree on the left side. That was a clear indication, to me, to go in that direction. Even if I made the wrong choice, it was better than wasting time standing in the same spot.

If I got lost, I could simply backtrack or improvise. Several additional red strings appeared farther ahead. This had to be the correct trail, I thought. Why else would someone put them there?

After an hour of pushing through the excruciating pain in my legs, I reached a clearing and saw a wooden house near the side of the trail. It stood on a flat, grassy surface, with a hill behind it. This was exactly what I needed, civilization. I'd ask someone for directions.

As I approached, three Nepalese kids ran out of the house and surrounded me.

"Candy, money, give, give," they yelled with their hands outstretched in front of them. They reminded me of three, young thugs in training. Their expressions didn't ask, but demanded. They wore dirty clothes, with more patches than I'd ever seen on any single piece of clothing.

The youngest boy, about five-years old, had enormous snot running down his nose, past his mouth and dripping down his chin, poor kid. The lack of medicine in remote, high-altitude locations often causes sinus complications.

In a flash, I remembered my friend's warning not to give away money, candy, or useless items to young children in Nepal. Instead, she suggested pens and notebooks to help them write. I looked at the rundown house and noticed an elderly woman giving me the evil eye through a broken window.

At that moment, I decided to give the kids candy. It did not seem as if they had it easy. They needed something to sweeten their lives. Of course, I didn't want to give them the candy for free. They had to earn their reward.

My map showed Mali to be the next village, about seven kilometers from Jiri. "Mali, where?" I asked the kids and pointed with my finger in the direction ahead.

"Mali, there, there!" The kids yelled excitedly and pointed in the same direction, and then they immediately chanted, "Candy, money, give."

Soon, I realized I wasn't the only person who'd ever asked for directions. Although I felt a little betrayed, it did not prevent me from giving them their just reward. I pulled out several candies from my pocket and handed each child two pieces. They unwrapped them, threw the paper covers on the ground and ate the delicious balls of sugar immediately. I hoped this wasn't their breakfast.

As I walked away, they yelled behind me, "More candy!"

Not long after, I entered the village of Mali, with its bustling size of three buildings and twenty-two-hundred-meter altitude. Despite the rundown houses, the wooden entrance doors had unique decorations varying from carvings to little trinkets attached to door handles and above the doorframe. This minute detail added charm, and I considered doing the same to my front door in Florida.

Atop the largest of the houses, proudly stood a familiar red communist flag, with a yellow hammer and sickle. Communism in Nepal? The owners of the house must have placed it there as a joke.

After confirming the route with a family working outside, I continued to follow the red strings to the next village called Shivalaya. The trail changed from heavy vegetation to open fields of grass, with an occasional pine tree and panoramic view of the scenery below.

To enter the town, I walked over my first suspended bridge, made out of metal and steel cables. Its length stretched for one hundred meters and offered a frightening view of the raging river below. I prepared my camera and photographed the crossing.

~*~*~

The large village of Shivalaya, situated alongside the Kali Gandaki River, boasted numerous restaurants and guest lodges to appease the travelers. Its size superseded Jiri.

As I walked through the town, I considered the various, small restaurants until I finally sat down at a table. A Nepalese woman greeted me and took my order.

Wanting to get back on the trail, I finished the beans, rice and pickled vegetables quickly. As I planned my day, I saw a young woman and a *Sherpa* coming closer. She seemed to be in her mid-twenties, with blond hair, wearing a pink shirt and a brown scarf around her neck. The Sherpa motioned for her to find a seat while he found the menu.

The young woman noticed me observing her and approached. "Hi, there. Can I join you?" She looked at me and smiled.

"I would be glad if you joined me. It's boring to sit alone, and good company is always welcome. My name is Aleksey."

She took a seat facing me. "My name is Seline. You speak good English, but you have an accent. Where are you from?"

"I'm from the United States but born in Russia. At the age of ten, I moved to the States with my family. I have the accent because I chose to keep it. I still remember a time during my junior high school days when a teacher asked me if I wished to lose the accent. I thought about it for moment, and replied, 'Nahhh!' It was one of the best choices I made in my life. I like accents, and it's a great conversation starter. Where are you from? I can't place it."

She laughed at my story. "You do have a nice accent. Don't change it. I'm from Switzerland and on my one-year trip around the world. Nepal is the last country before I go back home."

"Congratulations! Damn, one year is a long time. Are you tired of being on the road? Do you miss home?"

"I don't miss home one bit, but I do miss my family. I miss my parents and sister very much. In a month, when I'm home, we'll be spending a lot of time together. They'll be waiting for me at the airport. However, my parents are still upset with me for quitting a well-paid job and traveling around the world, alone."

"If you don't mind me asking, what was your job? Now that you are at the end of your journey, was it worth quitting?" I was curious about other peoples' life-changing decisions. Would her feelings mirror mine, or would she feel regret?

Up to this point, after talking to various travelers with similar situations, I had not yet met one person who regretted changing their life to traveling abroad. Would she be the first one to be different?

"Please, I don't mind if you ask. I'm happy to share my thoughts with another traveler. My friends, even my family, after a few minutes of listening to me talk about my adventures, start to feel bored. Not because they don't care, but because they can't relate to the experience. It's nice to talk to other travelers, because we understand each other and truly enjoy sharing our stories. I've learned a lot from listening to others as well.

"To answer your question, I have no regrets about quitting my job and traveling abroad. I worked as an accountant for a large company in Switzerland. It paid well, and I made wonderful friends. However, the job made me feel trapped. Every day I did the exact same thing. I wanted to live an exciting life, not be trapped sitting behind a desk all day counting numbers. I wasn't happy. I wanted to see the world. So, I saved thirty thousand francs, quit my job and went on a one-year journey around the world. It's the best decision I made in my life."

Her *Sherpa* returned and handed her a menu. She made a selection and gave it back.

I thought about her answer before replying. "Well done. You are a brave person to make such an important decision. It's not something most people would do in your situation. On a different note, what food did you order?"

"Oh, the usual, fried rice with bean soup and ginger tea. You?"

"The usual too, dal bhat, with garlic soup and ginger tea. The locals told me garlic soup helps the body acclimatize to altitude better, so I eat it every chance I get. Despite the garlic breath, I love the soup. I've also heard, ginger tea helps the circulation, thus, it also helps acclimatization. The tea is horrid. I force myself to drink the spicy liquid every time. The locals usually add extra-fresh ginger to my tea thinking they're doing me a favor, but I suffer every time."

At the very thought of ginger tea, I unintentionally shuddered. "So, what countries have you visited? Do any particular foods stand out?" I asked.

"From Switzerland, I went to the United States. Started with New York City and eventually made it to California, then Canada and South America. Afterward, I went to Southeast Asia. The most unique and tasty food was there. Vietnam, Laos, Thailand and Cambodia left a big impression on me. I think that's where I got the *intestinal parasite*." She said the last sentence softly, almost to herself.

"Are you sure it was a parasite? How did you get it treated?" I wondered, because eating weird, local foods was one of my most favorite experiences.

"Oh, I still have the parasite. At first, I simply thought I had an upset stomach, but after a month of light diarrhea and other symptoms, I went to the doctor. He identified the type of parasite I have and told me which pills to take. The medicine takes a while to work. I decided to wait until I get back to Switzerland. I'll take care of it then, with my doctor."

I laughed. "Wow, you're tough. Let me tell you a funny story about the weird foods I ate in Japan . . ." We talked for almost two hours, sharing stories and experiences.

In the end, we asked for the bill and waited at the table.

I enjoyed Seline's company and didn't want it to end so soon. "So, what's your plan from here? I know we're going the same way to the next village. Let's walk together, although you're probably in better physical shape than I am. I've barely exercised and may not be able to keep up with you after a few miles."

"Of course, let's walk together. It's fun to have company on a trail. I'm sure you're in good shape. You look fit and strong. Besides, I'm cheating a little bit. I have a Sherpa to carry my backpack and equipment and guide the way."

On our way out of Shivalaya, I confirmed my Gaurishankar Conservation Area permit with a man near the bridge at the end of the village. He explained the necessary payment for the permit to enter the park ahead. Afterward, Seline and I had to register with the police before exiting the village. The registration required us to enter a full name, passport number, date of birth and age, into a log.

I entered my information and moved away to let Seline register as well. She filled it out and started to walk away.

"Hey, young woman, you forgot to enter your age," the police officer called out.

I saw the anxious look on her face. She turned around and looked flustered, like a deer startled by headlights. "I don't want to enter my age. I entered the date of birth. That's enough," she protested.

"You have to put your age in the box here." He pointed. "How old are you?" He half smiled, as if he enjoyed making her say the age aloud.

"What? I don't want to say," she persisted.

I must admit. I now felt curious about her age, as well. She seemed young, but it was hard to tell.

"If you don't fill out the registration completely, I cannot let you through." The police officer's face displayed a stern look.

"Fine, I am thirty-two. There. Can I go now?" I could see a light crimson color on her cheeks as she turned around and walked toward me, without waiting for an answer from the officer.

Seline and I walked out of the village and onto a trail that led toward a mountain. Once we reached it, the trail changed. I took the lead. After five minutes of intense uphill climbing, I struggled for breath.

"Why don't you take the lead. I think I'll need to slow down a bit," I told Seline and her Sherpa. I tried so hard to keep up, but after another five minutes, I was out of breath again. A burning pain in my legs prevented me from going farther. I called out, "Seline, I need to take a break. You go on ahead. I'll try to catch up to you later."

"No problem. We all have our own pace. I'll see you soon or at the next village." She smiled and pushed on ahead.

I waved my hand and watched her climb.

At that moment, she stopped, turned around and added, "All this uphill is a great exercise for the butt. I'll be in great shape when I get back home." She smiled sweetly and continued walking uphill.

I couldn't help but steal a glance.

~*~*~

The rest of the day, I tried to catch up to Seline and followed the red markings on the trail. Fighting an uphill battle, I stopped every few minutes to rest. It felt like being on a rollercoaster, trekking up endless heights. Passing two smaller villages along the way did not persuade me to stop and explore them. I had to push on.

After several hours, the sunset convinced me to find a place for the night. Although I had my tent, I wanted to confirm the price of lodges. According to the map, a village called Bhandar lay ahead.

When I reached it, a group of kids were playing soccer. Behind them, the setting sun illuminated the field with its deep, orange colors. The kids ran around as the lingering daylight surrounded them. They were like little balls of fire, bright and full of energy.

I stood there for a moment and watched them. My backpack felt heavy. I wanted to take it off and play with them, but my body felt too tired. I continued along the trail and moments later, an advertisement for lodges guided the way. Exhaustion played a significant role in my decision making. The very first lodge, called Guest Lodge, enticed me to stay there.

I approached the two-story, stone building and knocked on the door. A Nepalese man greeted me and offered a room for three hundred rupees, a little over three US dollars. The price convinced me not to waste time setting up a tent. I asked for dinner and breakfast, but the family had already eaten and referred me to a nearby restaurant.

The lodge host took me to a simple room, with two made-up beds covered with heavy blankets. There were no other pieces of furniture, not even a chair. It sure beat sleeping outdoors.

As I sat down on the bed, I noticed spiders crawling in every part of the room, including the bed. I jolted up immediately. Upon closer examination, they appeared to be *daddy long-legs* about the size of my fist.

I felt relieved because I knew this spider was not harmful. *MythBusters* proved the common misconception of this arachnid, as extremely poisonous but unable to pierce the human skin, to be false. Supposedly, the poison was tested in a lab and proven to be weak. I could live with that, at least for one night. Due to the cold, I planned to sleep with my clothes on anyway.

I left my backpack in the room and ventured outside to find warm food. Only several houses in Bhandar showed the existence of electricity. After locating a brightly-lit lodge, I knocked on the door.

As I waited for an answer, I admired the unique woodwork on the doorframe. It seemed as if Nepal had a custom of decorating a door and its frame. Most doors were painted with natural colors like blue, green and even yellow, while the frames seemed to have various decorative carvings. It added charm and personality.

The noise of an opening door brought me back to reality. I explained my situation to the woman at the entrance in English, and she agreed to make dinner for me. Almost all the tables were filled with foreigners, who were eating and studying their *Lonely Planet guidebooks*.

When my large plate of dal bhat arrived, the woman asked me, "Why didn't you stay at our lodge? We have warm delicious food, a hot shower, comfortable beds and Wi-Fi."

I thought about her question and concluded it was because I didn't have the Lonely Planet guidebook. This brand, the largest travel guidebook publisher in the world, was commonly used by backpackers. I disliked it with a passion. Each time I saw someone looking at their guidebook, I felt provoked, even angry.

Not to degrade the readers, guidebooks are amazing. They offered helpful information, advertised local services and showed various routes to reach destinations safely. However, when I saw tourists using the guidebook at every turn to decide their restaurants, accommodations and calling it the "Bible of the Road", it saddened me.

In my opinion, when a traveler let a guidebook dictate their trip, it no longer became an adventure, but simply retraced the steps of someone else. It took away the mystery of the road, the unexpected, and set a standard of high expectations by merely promoting the popular. The romance of the road was then gone.

Getting lost in this world had already become difficult, and encountering the unexpected, extraordinary situations a subject to read about in adventure books, only to be mentioned as a safety hazard in guidebooks.

Once aware of the unexpected, can it still be called an adventure? My accommodation for the night may not have been the best, but at least I supported a different family and spread the wealth.

After dinner, I went back to the lodge, cleaned up with a moist towel and passed out under a heavy set of blankets, with daddy long-legs to keep me company. The day of trekking over twenty kilometers and the several thousand-meter adventure, left me exhausted. It had been a good decision to start the trek a week earlier to prepare my body for the climb ahead.

Chapter 8

In the morning, I ate an extra-large portion of garlic soup and leftover *dal bhat*, which the family offered as an extra. The soup looked funky and tasted like rotten vegetables that had been boiled for a long time to cover the flavor, but I needed energy.

After several hours of trekking, the increased difficulty was incomparable to the previous day. The elevation fluctuated several hundred meters at a time, continuously, until eventually reaching a new height of twenty-seven hundred meters, about eight thousand one hundred feet.

My body ached and I felt tired. As I sat on a rock and massaged my legs, I remembered today's cold, challenging trek. The higher I climbed, the more the scenery had changed. The vegetation grew barren and the villages more distant.

I now saw more peaks below the horizon than above. Enormous stones lay in all directions as if they had broken off from the top of a mountain and rolled downward. They stood tall and strong, like a noble king overlooking his land with an all-seeing eye.

In the distance, I saw several lodges and decided to stay at one of them for the night. The map indicated the location to be few kilometers past the village of Dakachu. Today I walked approximately twenty-two kilometers, about fourteen miles.

Approaching a two-story lodge alongside the trail, I noticed several busy foreigners outside. Among them, I saw Seline unpacking her backpack.

"Hi there," I called out.

She greeted me with a warm smile and we chatted away. I decided to stay in the same lodge and have dinner together but not before taking care of daily routine chores. Laundry awaited. As if on cue, the overcast sky cleared, and the sun warmed my fingers. Washing my unmentionables and socks by hand in freezing water proved to be an exhilarating experience.

In the evening, Seline and I got together and enjoyed the setting sun over another long conversation.

"I wondered if I'd see you again. After we parted ways, I waited for you at the next village but you didn't show," Seline said.

"That's weird. I took a few breaks but pushed on and made good distance. I know my pace can be slow at times, but I developed a new walking technique to help me make better time. I call it 'The Walking Dead'. It's perfect, really. With this technique, I can walk longer distances and save energy at the same time."

"'The Walking Dead?' Now that's entertaining. You piqued my interest. Could you please share your secret technique with me?" Seline giggled.

"OK. Here's what you do. When you go uphill, try to relax your body. Let your arms dangle on the sides without moving them. Walk at a slow, yet consistent pace. Relax your legs as much as possible, and lift them up as little as possible, almost dragging them along. Don't step on the big rocks, but concentrate on the smaller ones. Pay attention to your breathing, and if you start to lose breath, slow down the pace but keep moving. It may not look very graceful, but it's efficient. I practiced this all afternoon and was able to make significantly longer distances."

"That makes sense. Taking smaller steps and walking at a consistent pace. I'll share this with my boyfriend. He'll have a laugh."

"Well . . . that sounds nice. I didn't realize you had a boyfriend. He must miss you, being away so long." I felt a mixture of emotions, most leaned toward disappointment.

"It's not like that. We met in Southeast Asia. He's also traveling the world but for a longer time than I. When we're both done, we'll meet again."

"Speaking of Southeast Asia and the parasite you got there, I almost got a stomach flu today as well. The breakfast I had this morning looked and tasted weird, but I ate it anyway. In the afternoon, I felt like throwing up. Thank God for my grandma's medicine. She used to make me take these pills called *Biseptol*. I took two tablets earlier and felt better. I'll have to be more careful about what I eat. Speaking of food, I think our dinner should be ready soon. Let's go inside." I smelled the delicious aroma.

The solar panels did not generate enough energy during the day to support the lights inside the lodge. However, candles illuminated each table and warmed the atmosphere.

As Seline and I ate, several travelers joined us for conversation. We talked the night away over candlelight, sharing the troubles and tribulations of our climb. Our laughter filled the room and warmed the cold night, helping me to forget my aches and pains.

After dinner, Seline and I walked to our rooms, which were side by side.

As she stepped inside her room, she left the door ajar and looked at me for a long moment. I looked back into her blue eyes. Her lips curved into a light smile. "Good night, Aleksey." She slowly closed the door.

Heck, what does that mean? I was never good at reading signals. Oh well, time to go to sleep. Tomorrow, I knew, would be another difficult day.

Chapter 9

Despite the late departure, I still managed to leave ahead of Seline. Packing took priority. Every item had its place. This way I knew immediately if a piece of equipment needed attention. In this case, toilet paper ran short. A heavy sigh left my lips.

For me, toilet paper proved sacred. I used it for the toilet, fire starting, napkins and the most important, wiping my runny nose in the cold weather. When I used hard, recycled paper, after a few uses, it felt like sand paper and my nose swelled from irritation. For me, it were the little things in life that made a big difference.

It seemed as if Nepal had a very limited amount of toilet paper outside the big cities. Not only was it an expensive, luxury item, it was customary, in Nepal, to use the left hand for cleaning after defecation. Because of this, I tried to eat with my right hand to show respect and packed extra toilet paper to avoid a catastrophe.

In the United States, *Boy Scouts of America* used various techniques to adapt to the lack of toiletries in case of an emergency. In the past, I had the privilege to be educated in their ways of outdoors toilet survival.

When toilet paper ran short, leaves were the next best alternative. Being aware of the poisonous trees helped immensely. In more severe situations, smooth stones worked almost as well. As a last alternative, a smooth stick worked wonders. I thanked my lucky stars for not having to resort to any of these replacements, and I didn't want to start now.

After an hour of climbing, I watched Seline pass me by.

"Yep, you go on ahead. I'll catch up to you later," I said, breathing heavily.

The day proved challenging, but my body impressed me the most. With the help of "The Walking Dead" technique, and quick adaptability of my body, I didn't stop as often.

Instead of watching other people pass by, I overtook most trekkers and locals alike. The only difficulty seemed to be the progression of cold weather. It aggravated my cough and made it difficult to wake up in the morning.

After several thousand meters of ups and downs, I caught up to Seline. We walked together to the next village called Junbesi. The charming village was mostly concentrated alongside the trail. The lodges varied in quality, from conservative options to more luxurious. Her Sherpa recommended the later and we went inside.

"I'll stay here today and tomorrow. Bibek, my Sherpa, will show me around the village tomorrow and take me to a nearby Buddhist temple. I'll also take a break from walking. What's your plan?" Seline asked.

"Staying here sounds nice, but I want to push on. The sun is still up and the road is calling, although, I can't tell on my map if there are any guesthouses in the next ten kilometers. I'll see as I go. Possibly, I'll use my tent. It's about time. Thank you, Seline, I've truly enjoyed spending time with you. I hope we'll see each other again."

"I have no doubt we'll meet again. You are stronger each time I see you. I won't be surprised if I see you coming back from Everest when I'm still on the way up."

I laughed, "I doubt it, but I'll look forward to seeing you again."

"Let me ask Bibek if he can help you with directions."

After chatting with the Sherpa, I better understood the climb ahead. I hugged Seline and prepared to leave.

"You don't have to walk so much, you know? The evening is approaching soon. You should stay."

I looked at her and almost changed my mind. "I know it's best if I stay, but I feel the need to keep moving."

"Alright, but you take care of yourself. If it gets too difficult, come back. You hear me?"

I smiled. "I hear you."

~*~*

As I walked out of the village, my doubts slowed me down. The evening approached and heavy clouds surrounded me. I felt disheartened, and the conviction of pushing onward waned, as did my strength after such a long day. Only the strong wind at my back pushed me forward, the same cold wind that bit my cheeks and numbed my skin.

Why did I leave? Am I truly pushing forward or simply running away? I wondered. It made no sense to go on. But then again, I came here to explore the mountains and better understand my limits. I couldn't stop now. Besides, I felt it would be too embarrassing to return.

After half an hour, reality set in. I felt cold, hungry and had no clear idea of where to sleep. The terrain didn't offer a convenient, flat camping spot. Not a single person passed by to ask for directions.

There were fewer trees now, with rocks and cliffs on all sides. The uphill climb made me sweat despite the freezing gusts of wind. The worst scenario would be getting into my sleeping bag sweaty. I took off my jacket and zipped up my wool fleece, which the wind easily blew through.

I sniffled and felt warm liquid run down my nose. My hand wiped away the fluids, and I immediately stopped to look at the blood on my fingers. The cold, dry air must have aggravated my nostrils. I continued pushing forward.

Once the sun had set and the darkness drew near, I started to worry. Then, I saw a two-story house in the distance. A nearby sign showed Everest Lodge. I approached the door and knocked. An older Nepalese woman greeted me in English and let me in.

The whole first floor was one large room. A hot furnace stood in the center, with piles of dung beside it, along with several logs. I saw the kitchen in the corner, and beds hugged the walls on the opposite side of the room. Several small wooden tables and chairs stood near the furnace. Three gray-haired men stared at me while warming up their hands.

The Nepalese woman said to pick any available bed and she'd serve dinner within an hour. I nodded in agreement and walked toward the three familiar Russian-speaking men. We had taken the same bus from Kathmandu to Jiri.

"I'm surprised to see you three here. I thought I made good distance, but you passed me by." I said in Russian.

The tallest of the three men spoke. "When we got off the bus in Jiri, we didn't stay there and pushed on to the next village."

His choice surprised me. "That's a great idea. I stayed in Jiri that night with a family. After that, I trekked fast but got lost a few times. The red markers on the trees helped immensely. Without them, it would have been more difficult."

The man laughed. "You mean the red strings on the trees? Those were put there for the upcoming running race. The race route is usually the longer and more difficult way to get to the next village."

"Well, damn. Now everything makes sense. No wonder Seline and I missed each other the other day. Oh well, I'll think of this as extra exercise to prepare myself for the passes ahead."

When I sat next to the three men, a kitten jumped on my lap, purred and rubbed against my arm. She looked skinny, even with all the white, fluffy fur. The black spots on the tip of her tail and left eye reminded me of a cat from my youth. After the kitten found a comfortable spot on my lap, she closed her eyes.

"I guess I make a warm blanket. I like cats," I mused aloud.

"I like dogs better. You won't find a more loyal companion. Why don't you join us for a drink and snacks? We have several bottles of vodka here. It's a great way to warm up before dinner." The oldest of the three smiled and showed me a bottle of Smirnoff, the largest vodka brand in the world.

Russians and vodka, no wonder people connected the two.

"I'll be happy to join you for a glass."

Eventually, the dinner arrived. We ate and prepared for bed. I kept my clothing on and tucked myself inside the sleeping bag. I zipped it up and pulled the string to cover my face but left a small hole for my mouth. My nose was useless from the congestion and didn't need to be exposed. Sleep overtook me immediately.

Chapter 10

I opened my eyes and gasped for breath. I tried to move. Why couldn't I move? In a state of panic, I frantically moved my arms. I needed air. The sleeping bag covered my face. Where was the damn zipper? I gasped harder, but there was so little air. I twisted and turned. Where was that damn zipper? I found it and yanked hard. The zipper got caught on the material and jammed halfway, but there was enough room to wriggle free.

My arms burst out from the sleeping bag. Saliva dripped from my mouth with each hard breath, and snot ran from my nose due to the congestion. I sat up and removed the sleeping bag from my eyes—nothing but darkness welcomed me. I yanked off my hat, jacket and scarf. I felt better but needed more air. I pushed down the sleeping bag, then felt for my water bottle, found it by the bed, unscrewed the cap and lifted it to my mouth. Only a few drops trickled out, followed by the familiar crackling sound of ice. The water had frozen.

I stood up, stumbled toward the door and pushed. It flung open. A freezing gust of wind slammed into my face, but it was what I wanted, what I needed. Immediately, I felt a sense of relief.

I simply stood in the same spot outside as I labored for breath. It took several minutes before my breathing calmed down, and then, in an instant, I noticed the biting cold. My fingers were numb, and my nose and cheeks prickled with pain. I started to shiver and went back inside.

When I stepped in, I heard the familiar snoring from the three men. It felt like I'd almost died, and they'd slept right through it—so selfish.

Oh well, I felt better. It was time to go back to sleep.

~*~*~

The first rays of the sun awakened me. A piercing light penetrated the frost-covered window and landed on my face. I crawled out of the sleeping bag and took in the gentle warmth with pleasure. The magical moment lasted for several minutes until I got tired of it.

My three roommates were still asleep, evident from their loud, wall-shaking snoring. Getting out of the warm bed was almost impossible but couldn't be avoided. After several basic stretches, I went to use the outdoor toilet.

As I stood in the outhouse, feeling the pressure lessen, the moment felt perfect. The Everest Lodge lived up to its name. I admired Mount Everest far in the distance through a small window on one side of the outhouse.

Despite the difficult night, I felt happiness. I'd searched for such moments. I didn't mean the toilet, but the sense of being. I knew this was exactly where I wanted to be.

I enjoyed the view a bit longer and realized this had to be the most enlightening bathroom experience of the journey. If only I could capture these moments in a bottle and sell them, the world would be a happier place.

When I walked out, I looked back and admired the outhouse from a distance. Mount Everest and various snow-capped giants made a grand background. All of a sudden, I had an epiphany. I knew I had to travel the rest of the world in search of the most scenic outhouses, take photos and write a book about them. It would be a unique approach, and fun.

Such great revelations made me hungry. I went back inside the lodge with a smile. The hostess made the biggest breakfast I'd had in Nepal yet. Afterward, I packed and made my way to a large village called Nunthala, where I planned to buy a new charger for my electronics.

My *Steripen Freedom* proved to be an amazing piece of equipment. Its length was the same as my index finger and used ultraviolet light to kill bacteria in water. Although it didn't filter, after spinning it for forty-eight seconds in half a liter of water, it cleared the harmful bacteria. Despite its redeeming qualities, it needed recharging after about fifty uses. All of my electronics charged via USB.

I first arrived at the town of Ringmu. It stood at the height of twenty-two hundred meters. Then I pushed on to Nunthala. All of the buildings and businesses aligned along the main road.

To my surprise, several locals stood behind small tables selling wares. The items sold were practical instead of souvenirs that usually served only one purpose. I saw telephone chargers, light bulbs, electricity converters and the like.

The idea of staying the night in Nunthala enticed me, but I still had energy to go farther. This journey was not a vacation to stop and enjoy the scenery but a competition with myself. How far could I go? How hard could I push myself?

On my way out, I found a place to eat. There I talked to the owner of a small restaurant.

"Are you married?" she asked, then sat across from me.

"No, I'm not married." After I answered, I saw a proud, almost arrogant smile form on the restaurant owner's face.

"That's too bad. I married a man from England. We have two children. How old do you think I am?"

I looked at her and studied her face. She seemed about thirty-five. Her skin appeared smoother than most other Nepali women her age that I'd seen. I didn't want to be rude. "You look around twenty-five."

That proud smile appeared again, followed by a quick rise of her nose. I felt like she wanted to climb on a pedestal and look down on me.

"That's nice of you to say. I'm thirty. My husband is in England and I work here. In a few months, I'll be with him again. You should get married as well. Find a nice Nepalese woman. We are great cooks and will make many children."

Did she just say that? "Uh, thank you. I'll think about it. How much will it be for the food?" I decided to make my way out before she offered me a mail-order bride.

After an interesting encounter with the restaurant owner, and then purchasing a charger, I continued toward Kharikhola, the village ahead. The map showed my journey there to be several thousand meters of many vicissitudes. The newly formed blisters on my feet disagreed with the long trek, but I wanted to walk a good distance today.

Kharikhola, a larger village located at the height of twenty-two hundred meters, had a small temple with a *Buddhist prayer wheel*, a telephone and a run-down medical facility that didn't appear operational. The dirty walls and broken window dissuaded me from taking a closer look.

As I walked through the village, I admired its placement. It stood on top of a mountain overlooking the valleys that surrounded it. I selected the most welcoming and brightest guesthouse, out of a vast selection of three, and knocked.

A Nepalese man opened the door and glanced at my backpack. "Welcome. Come in, come in. I'll take you to your room. You must be tired from today's climb. Settle in and I'll have my wife cook you a warm meal." The man smiled and waved his hand for me to follow.

"Thank you. How much for the night?" Hard-earned experience taught me to ask the price before accepting any accommodations.

"Five hundred rupees for the room and six hundred more for dinner and breakfast. I'll have my wife pack a lunch for you as well. Where did you come from today?"

I calculated the full price to be about seven US dollars. "I think I started somewhere near Junbesi."

"That's not a distance a trekker usually climbs in one day. Well done. Follow me to the room." He opened a door. "This is your room. Key and lock are on the table. Food will be ready soon. Don't go far."

"Thank you. You are a good host. Do you have a bucket I can use to wash my clothing?"

He smiled again. "No problem. I'll have a bucket ready for you in the kitchen. You can use the hose outside for the water."

As I hand washed my clothing in the freezing water, I admired the sunset. Some of my friends claimed sunsets were the same everywhere. The sun rose and then it set. Colors were beautiful but orange was still orange and red was still red no matter where they looked at it.

I disagreed. Even in the same location, every sunset looked unique. On clear days, I saw the beautiful ever-changing sun color everything in its luster. Like a blanket of light, it shone upon everything unbiased.

Formerly, I remembered some clouds resembling puffy, cotton candy, with deep, colorful pinks and reds. I always enjoyed watching them slowly drift away and change into different puppets. This was such an evening, an evening of colors and shapes.

After laundry, I wanted nothing more than to eat and fall asleep, but the necessity of daily preparations took precedence. In addition to organizing my equipment, shaving and studying the map for the next day, I had to drain my newly formed blisters and apply medicine. Success was not about luck but persistence and structure.

In the kitchen, I met my host and joined him for dinner. He turned on the television and flipped through different channels. The big antenna outside was not just for show. He stopped at the only English-speaking channel. It showed a *World Wrestling Entertainment* match.

He laughed. "Wow, look at those two midgets fighting against the big man. What a fierce match. I wouldn't want to be their opponent. This must happen a lot in America."

I smiled and remained silent.

Chapter 11

The alarm buzzed and jolted me awake. I slammed my hand against the phone screen to silence the loud thing and went back to sleep. I deserved a good night's rest and immediately decided to trek less today. Unfortunately, once awoken, I wasn't able to fall back asleep. The thought of getting closer to my goal enticed me to get up.

I stepped out of the lodge and pushed on like the walking dead, weary eyed and dragging my feet. After a few minutes, the food in my stomach energized me and I pushed on with greater zeal.

After half a day of trekking, Paiya stood in the distance. I appreciated the little village. Initially, I'd planned to spend the night and catch up with my journal writing but considered moving on after filling up my belly.

My stomach protested and I sat outside at a three table-sized restaurant. Looking around, I saw several brick guest-houses with colorful metal roofs far in the distance. Most lodges were also restaurants and had outdoor seating, like the one I was in.

Colorful *Tibetan prayer flags* hung from the roofs and fluttered about. Normally, this would have made a heavenly lunch spot, but the bleak environment set a darker mood. Mountains surrounded Paiya on all sides, and ominous, dark clouds slowly descended.

After ordering, I didn't want to wait for my food alone and started a conversation with the only other person, a bearded young backpacker sitting at the other table.

"You're coming back? How far up did you go? What's your plan from here?" I asked, curious to hear about his experience.

"I reached Gokyo Point and stayed there for the night but couldn't go farther. I started to get signs of altitude sickness and turned back. It did a number on me. The severe headache, shortness of breath, loss of energy and appetite worried me. The glacier beyond Gokyo was tricky, and I didn't have crampons to cross. The highest I reached was forty-eight hundred meters, about fourteen thousand feet." The young backpacker grimaced. "How far do you plan to go today?" he asked.

"I think I'll stay here tonight and start early tomorrow to get to Namche, and then stay two nights there to acclimatize. I've been walking too much and have a whole bunch of new blisters. The altitude is also a problem for me. I'm moving up in elevation too rapidly."

"It'll be very difficult to make it in one day to Namche from here. I recommend you go farther today," he suggested.

"Thank you for the advice. It seems like I'll have to wait until Namche to take a break. I hope our food arrives soon. All this walking is really making me hungry. I eat like a racehorse. I stuff myself with rice and beans until I can't eat anymore, but after three hours, I'm starving again. Damn, my stomach is a bottomless pit that demands food. No amount can satisfy it for long," I complained.

"I'm the same, but I find the cold more troublesome."

I quoted, "'. . . it's cold out there today. It's cold out there every day.' *Groundhog Day*, with *Bill Murray*. Love that movie."

"Haven't seen it. I can't wait to get back home. Nepal is a difficult country. Everything is dirty. I miss my comforts."

"I miss home as well," I confessed. "But glad to be released from the addiction of daily comforts. Now, I embrace the simplicity of living in the moment, without a care for tomorrow. Simply speaking, I have no time to worry. On a trip like this, it's one day at a time. I don't worry about the next bill or the loans I have to pay. I only worry about where I'll sleep tonight, where to eat and where it hurts so I can patch it up. I enjoy this lifestyle," I explained.

He grumbled, "I felt the same at the beginning. After a while though, I got tired of all this. The novelty of being hungry and cold on a beautiful mountain is old to me now. Although there is a certain kind of peace here, I always have a purpose, like putting one foot in front of the other. That's about as complicated as it gets. It's a simple, honest yet consuming action. It gives me time to think."

I thought about his answer for a moment. "I don't know about the novelty of hunger and cold, but I agree with giving you time to think things through. When I walk for hours, days, or weeks at a time, I don't find it boring. My mind wanders from thought to thought, freely, without disturbance. It's almost as if my brain is sorting itself out, then after the process, I feel refreshed. Troubles become simpler. Thoughts become clearer and make more sense."

He laughed. "You sound like a computer hard drive defragging."

"That sounds about right. However, I believe that living too comfortably can be exhausting for the mind. Having everything leads to boredom and then depression. I need a break from the city life sometimes to do a reality check and appreciate the comforts I have."

I sighed and continued, "I think that many people in developed countries have lost their purpose in life. Going about the daily rat race, climbing that corporate ladder and repressing their desires until they eventually go crazy. I feel that going back to the basics of day-to-day living can unburden them from trying to find that picture-prefect life and the exhausting road to perfection. In third world countries, people are too busy trying to feed their families rather than worrying about the purpose of their lives.

"Too many people are now looking for that perfect answer from a psychologist or taking that prescription pill to make their sadness go away. In a poor country, your psychologists are the all-knowing old grandmas, who spend their days sitting on benches outside their houses collecting all the gossip they can. Their life experiences will set most people straight in a moment."

He laughed again. "Wow, it looks like you really thought this through."

I laughed too. "I guess I did. Or maybe this is the excuse I came up with to spend my vacations like this." Our food arrived and we dug in.

I stopped eating for a moment and looked at my half-empty plate. The rice and beans were almost gone, but the three, small pieces of cheese lay in the corner untouched like a treasure.

I smirked and couldn't help but share my thoughts. "You know, when I'm on the road with a limited budget, I somehow always keep the best part of the meal for last so that I can appreciate it and savor the moment. Back home, with plenty of options, I dig in and eat the best parts first and leave the undesired unfinished. Oh, how the circumstances have changed."

"I don't know what you're talking about. I always keep the best piece for last." To prove his point, he intentionally moved a desired piece of food to a corner of his plate, then we shared several more travel stories.

After lunch, I pushed on to one of several lodge-sized villages called Surke. There I found a cheap guesthouse for the night. Before I fell asleep, I realized the foreigner and I hadn't exchanged names or mentioned where we were from. That often happened on the road. People connected for a moment, and then moved on like ships in the night.

Chapter 12

The days were getting colder due to the rise in elevation. I left the guesthouse at sunrise to make it to Namche Bazaar by late afternoon, and then planned to take an early break.

Along the way, I passed a large village called Lukla. It had an airport. Most visitors and climbers used this small airport to get to this region. Paul, the young businessman who helped me in Kathmandu, scheduled a flight for me to leave Lukla at the end of my journey. I planned to explore this village then.

The number of tourists drastically increased once I passed Lukla. So did the number of lodges and snack stalls along the way. I took advantage of the cheaper prices of Snickers bars and bought fifteen of them. The total cost was three thousand rupees, about thirty-six US dollars.

Snickers offered a large number of calories, and the fast absorbing sugar energy helped on the trail, thus making it expensive. I called it "survival food." Chocolate bars were not a staple food at home, but I savored them on the road.

By late afternoon, I approached the entrance of Namche Bazaar, or simply Namche as the locals called it. People of all ages filled the ascending road. Men and women with colorful backpacks laughed and took photographs of every house and unique signs. Most of them disregarded the courtesy of asking the locals for a photograph and simply photographed without regard. I didn't judge them because I did the same.

As I stepped into the large village of Namche, I paused to take in the panoramic view. It looked like a deep horseshoe canyon with many terraces. The village almost reminded me of the Vietnamese rice fields but instead of rice on each terrace, there were buildings and roads that zigzagged to the top. Namche had more infrastructure than any village I'd seen since I started the climb.

As I walked through the village looking for a lodge, numerous people walked along the streets. Small outdoor and indoor stores stood on all sides and corners. The products ranged from chocolate bars, clothing, and climbing equipment, to simple souvenirs. I'd decided to shop for necessities later.

After comparing prices with several desirable lodges, I chose one that stood relatively close to the center of Namche. The owner seemed friendly. I unpacked in my room, and then went out to explore. Despite my small budget, I had a strong desire to treat myself to different foods, other than rice and beans.

The village center offered a German bakery, pizza restaurant and my favorite, a donut shop. I couldn't resist a slice of pizza and a donut. The price of these two items could buy me four local dinners, but I needed a change.

I sat down at a table in the pizza restaurant and stared at my prized food. My mouth salivated in anticipation. I slowly picked up a slice and bit off a piece, closing my eyes to savor the moment.

After several chews, I realized something was amiss. It didn't taste like pizza but a wet piece of bread with dry cheese. I looked closer and noticed hardly any tomato sauce. A tear almost ran down my cheek.

The donut still gave me hope, but after a few bites, it wasn't any better. It tasted dry and bland. I felt disappointed after having spent so much money. Later, I entered a local hole-in-the-wall restaurant and ordered rice and beans with garlic soup. I knew I wouldn't be disappointed.

When the sun had set, I returned to the lodge and entered my cold room without counting the number of days I hadn't taken a shower. The price of one bucket of hot water was equivalent to about five dinners. Besides, the cold weather worked like a refrigerator and kept my body well preserved. I went to sleep early to recover my strength and prepare for the climb ahead.

Chapter 13

The morning greeted me with a persistent headache and a sore throat. Despite this, I had a plan for the day. Climbing higher and then returning to a lower elevation on the same day was commonly known to help acclimatization. In addition, I also wanted to explore the area around Namche.

After breakfast, I didn't take a map and climbed the trail behind Namche to explore the vicinity ahead. At first, I thought I felt tired, but after a few minutes, I realized the challenges of the altitude. I had no energy and every step felt as if I had run a marathon. I felt drained and out of breath.

When I failed to take a break every minute or two, the fatigue made breathing exhausting. The higher I climbed, the more difficult it became. By the time I reached a clearing, I didn't think I could go farther. Even the thought of crawling up-hill seemed more appealing, but then I remembered that real men don't quit halfway. I pushed on.

Half an hour more at a turtle-crawling pace, the popular Everest View Hotel stood at the height of three thousand eight hundred and eighty meters, about eleven thousand feet.

It commanded my attention because there were no other structures on the hill. The large, delicate glass windows and me-ticulous brickwork of the building enticed me to go inside. As a foreigner, I wouldn't be seen as a solicitor.

The interior had class and offered well-polished wooden walls with decorative photographs of locals. Large windows in the restaurant highlighted the amazing view of Mount Everest. I now felt numb looking at the Mountain. However, the sign at the front desk truly stole my heart. "Hot Showers in Every Room—Wi-Fi Included."

Despite my tight budget, the desire for a hot shower over-whelmed me. I approached the man at the front desk and flashed my most charming smile. "Hi. Could you please tell me the price of your least expensive room for the night?"

The front desk agent wore a white, long-sleeved shirt and a black vest. He answered politely, "The cheapest room for the night is one hundred and forty US dollars. We only have two of these rooms left. It also comes with a hot shower and complementary Wi-Fi. Would you like to stay for the night?"

I stood there in silence for a moment and calculated the amount of dinners I could buy with that money. After a shocking result, I thanked the man and got back on the trail.

Far in the distance, I saw a cluster of buildings and made them my next destination. The degree of elevation lessened and made it easier for me to make better time. Upon arrival, a sign greeted me, "Welcome to Kumjing."

Mountains surrounded the village and offered a scenic view in all directions. The clear-blue sky and the warm rays of the sun made it seem like a charming, quaint village.

Most of the houses had tall stone walls around each property. The little streets felt like a maze without a pattern or direction. I ran into dead ends and had to backtrack several times.

The village seemed unnaturally empty. In spite of the number of houses, I didn't see a single person or hear sounds of civilization. I followed the deserted streets until I reached a Buddhist temple. The gates were open and I stepped inside.

On the right I saw a one-story sized prayer wheel and on the left a garden. After several minutes of exploring the temple grounds, it felt eerie not seeing a single monk.

Despite the quaint beauty of the village, it lacked life and failed to entice me to stay longer. On the way back, I saw several tables filled with trinkets for sale, with prices listed next to the items. However, there were no people to take the money. Weren't they afraid someone would steal their wares? I walked faster to find my way out of the village.

Kumjing left a lasting impression on me. After forty-five minutes of exploration, I felt depressed. A city without people felt like a theme park without children. There was no joy. What purpose did it serve? Maybe the locals worked in Namche during the day.

Walking back downhill didn't pose a challenge, and my speed increased considerably. Once I went over a hill and saw Namche in the distance, I stopped and sat down to enjoy the view.

I saw a hotel called Hotel Hill-Ten. After counting the hills, it was indeed located on hill number ten. Alternatively, they could have meant Hilton. Regardless, I found it funny and took a photo.

Namche stood at the center of a large hill. On a different hill to its left, I saw a helicopter slowly landing on a helipad. The hill to its right had a military base, with soldiers actively training. After enjoying the scenery, I continued my descent.

On my way back, I ate a Snickers bar and then went on a mission to satisfy my craving for cheesecake. The rest of the day I explored Namche and ate random foods. To my surprise, the cheesecake tasted delicious and improved my mood. In the evening, snowflakes started to fall and persuaded me to return to my lodge.

~*~*~

As I waited in the kitchen for my dinner, I began a conversation with Sarah, one of the guests. She looked to be in her sixties and had short, silver hair.

Sarah looked worried. "I couldn't reach the Base Camp and had to stop at Gokyo Point. The altitude sickness forced me to return. Jon, my Sherpa, helped me come back here yesterday."

"Good job making it that far. I'm glad you made it here safely, though. What altitude sickness symptoms did you experience?" I felt curious to learn from her experience.

"The loss of energy was the first sign. After that, I lost my appetite and always had a severe headache. My husband, Richard, fared better than I and stayed with Kamal, our second Sherpa, and tried to go farther." She looked out the window with worry. The snow fell at an increasing pace.

I also glanced outside. "I hope the snowfall won't be too heavy. I plan to leave tomorrow. Don't worry too much about your husband. Based on your description of him, he sounds like a tough man. Your other Sherpa is also with him." I tried to comfort her.

A moment of silence replaced the conversation. I continued to look out the window and enjoyed watching the snow fall. The drastic change of weather excited me. It offered a challenge. I looked forward to the thrilling experience of sleeping in my tent surrounded by mountains and snow. Not using my tent felt like a waste this past week.

After dinner, I joined Jon and a group of other Sherpas for a game of cards. The game rules were easy to learn. As we played, we talked about altitude sickness and inexperienced climbers.

Jon, Sarah's Sherpa, complained, "We've had so many accidents this year. Visitors underestimate altitude and suffer consequences. Many climbers believe their excellent fitness level will prevent altitude sickness, but this is not true. The most common location for sickness is here, in Namche."

Jon continued, "I often see fit and energetic young people land in Lukla airport, which is just fourteen kilometers south of here. They immediately start climbing to reach Namche where the elevation is three thousand four hundred and fifty meters, which is a bit over eleven thousand feet. By the time they reach Namche, or during their sleep, many suffer from altitude sickness. The small hospital here is always packed with foreigners. I win." Jon placed his winning hand on the table.

"This is the second time you won in a row. What's your secret?" I wondered.

Jon laughed, "OK, OK, I'll share the trick with you. Here is what—"

The door to the kitchen slammed opened and a Nepalese man rushed in. He looked around until his gaze fell on Sarah and Jon. "Sarah, Richard is in the hospital. He's got altitude sickness but is doing better now. He still has difficulty recognizing people and—"

"What? Take me to him." Sarah quickly got out of the chair, picked up her jacket and left with Kamal and Jon.

One of the Sherpas at the table commented, "Richard will probably be fine. Medicine works fast and he's at a lower altitude now. This type of altitude sickness is the most difficult, though. It has different stages, and the last stage is complete confusion. Richard's state of mind won't be different from a child's. It's good that Kamal took him back early enough before it got worse."

"That sounds scary. I can't imagine going to sleep . . . and not waking up. I wish the best for Richard. What do you say we finish our game? I think I'll win this one." With Jon gone, I felt confident.

After the game, I went back to my room and lay in bed thinking about the evening. The effects of altitude sickness were more severe than I imagined. I now understood the reason people went in groups and hired Sherpas. It was for safety, but I still desired to continue without a guide. The higher the risk, the greater the thrill.

~*~*~

As I lay in bed trying to fall asleep, my thoughts wandered to the wonderful people I'd met in Nepal and the unique foods I ate. How will I remember these moments six months from now? I wasn't sure, but the memories from last year's adventure in Ireland finally took shape.

Although many memories of Ireland faded away, some became significant. They filtered and were a bag of mixed emotions. I recalled a fulfilling moment during my first visit to Glendalough, a small village on the east side of Ireland.

There I remembered walking toward a lake with mountains surrounding me on all sides. The strong winds ruffled my hair. In the distance, a flowing river made its way down a valley with dark clouds reflecting the somber mood in the still puddles.

Winds agitated the lake and created a rhythm in the waves. They crashed onto the shoreline almost reaching my boots every time, yet as if to their disappointment were always a minute distance from their goal. I stood there, letting the wind embrace me. The cold gusts bit my skin and numbed my cheeks.

Pure joy radiated from my heart.

I'd searched the world for such a moment. The countless, insignificant details came together and made it perfect. After a little while, I left Glendalough.

Little did I realize I would return. There I made friends and lifelong memories, but I had never seen the same kind of waves at the lake again.

This was a happy memory of Ireland. Each time I recalled the moment, it filled me with a sense of wonder and fulfillment. However, not all memories were as pleasant. Some left me with regret.

Like the day I went with a friend on a boat trip to an island off the coast of west Ireland. Two girls we'd met the day before joined us. Upon our arrival, we rented bicycles and rode together.

At some point, I separated from the group and stood at a fork in the road, lost in thought. I heard a woman's voice calling out behind me. I turned around and saw her pull over on a bicycle.

"Follow me. I'll show you the right way," she said.

I saw a happy and hopeful look in her eyes. As we rode side by side, I noticed a beautiful autumn leaf tattoo on her arm. It complimented her. We didn't say much. There was no need to. It felt comfortable.

Before I realized, we caught up to my friends and I saw them in the distance. The two girls waved for me to come their way. I turned around and found the girl with the autumn leaf looking at me. I watched her eyes, full of hope and happiness, change to hurt and sadness.

I stood rooted in place and watched her take a different path away from me. I wanted to call out and say, "It's not what you think," and explain, but I didn't. The deciding moment was soon gone and regret followed, leaving nothing but a memory. Why didn't I say anything? Was I not confident enough? Was it something else?

I still didn't know the answer. All I knew was that every time I remembered my best and my worst moments, my mind changed it just a little until these memories became my biggest illusions, occasionally surfacing to beckon me.

As I lay in bed in Namche, remembering Ireland, the cold air enveloped me. I almost got up to get a third blanket but couldn't manage to leave the bed's lingering, warm embrace. I lay still and wondered. What memories will I create in Nepal?

Chapter 14

I looked out the window to appreciate a hint of orange highlighting the snowy mountaintops. Sometime during the night, the snow stopped falling. A soft, white blanket completely covered the streets of Namche. I packed and left the lodge to start a new day.

How far would I climb today? I didn't know, but knew I wouldn't rush. Climbing too fast would cause altitude sickness. The recommended safe altitude gain was three hundred to five hundred meters per day. Anything more invited trouble.

Last night's snowfall covered the trail and beautified the surroundings. I climbed in the shadows of the snow-capped mountains. The sun glowed behind their uneven edges.

An occasional ray of sun found its way through an opening of the high rises and lit up a path in front of me. The playful sun rays made unique shadow puppets in all shapes and sizes. I let my imagination run wild and enjoyed the moment.

I expected the heavy weight of my backpack to be an issue, but it wasn't. Despite the slight headache, I gained elevation with ease. By the time I gained five hundred meters from Namche, I decided to push farther.

By afternoon, I arrived at the village of Dhole. There were only several buildings, but colorful clothing hung outside every window. It must have been laundry day. Atop each roof stood a bright, red communist flag, with a hammer and sickle drawn on it. Was this an ongoing local joke, or were these people serious? I found it difficult to believe that Nepal had anything to do with communism.

Dhole stood at the height of almost forty-one hundred meters. I had climbed twice the recommended altitude gain for the day. Out of the two available lodges, I chose Yeti Lodge because it was the closest and cleanest building around.

The moment I stepped into the room and sat on the bed fatigue washed over me. I did not want to stay in my small, dark room otherwise I would have fallen asleep. Instead, I made my way to the warm lounge area. It had a working metal stove in the center. I sat on a chair and wrote in my journal about today's events.

Before bed, I took an aspirin to help my headache. It also thinned the blood and relieved stress on the heart.

Chapter 15

Another day, another sunrise. I hit the trail again. As a stranger, whom I met several days ago, said, "I simply put one foot in front of the other." My cellphone had sufficient battery power so I listened to music. The cheerful song "I Miss You" by the pop punk band Blink 182, helped take my mind off the aches and pains in my legs.

I put the song on replay and continued to climb. The questions about life troubled me. Like, why did the band Blink 182 break up? Couldn't they stay together and make more great music? Or, why was I farting so much? Could these farts propel me to climb faster? I guessed some questions didn't have immediate answers.

After several hundred meters of elevation gain, I met a Polish couple going the same way. They seemed to be around my age, mid-twenties. We enjoyed a conversation and reached a village called Machhermo in a valley at the height of forty-four hundred meters. There were six, one-story houses clustered together and two more in the distance.

The Polish couple and I chose to stay at the same lodge. After inspecting my room, I left the equipment and went back on the trail to climb higher before sleep. In the distance, I saw a worn trail going up a steep, rocky hill. Tibetan prayer flags marked the summit.

Without the weight of the backpack, I started at a good pace. I climbed a hundred meters, and then felt the onset of the burning pain in my legs. Every additional step felt more arduous. After climbing a hundred meters more, the severe headache almost made me turn back, but I persevered.

The colorful Tibetan prayer flags ruffled in the wind, as if calling out to me. I admired them until the winds grew stronger. It seemed as though the rope holding the flags would tear at any moment. I knew I had to reach the top. There was no turning back. The pain didn't matter, only the next step did.

The summit was only fifty meters farther. Hard breaths followed every step I took. I no longer breathed through my nose but opened my mouth and took in fast gulps of cold air. I stumbled and fell on one knee but immediately stood up. This damned hill wouldn't get the better of me.

I took the final step, reached the summit and held onto the rope of the prayer flags for stability. There was no joy, no emotions, just hard breaths and a sharp pain in my head. I didn't stay and immediately descended. My watch showed a total elevation gain of three hundred meters.

At the lodge kitchen, several tables with chairs took up most of the space. Other than the female Nepalese owner who greeted me, there was no one around. I asked for hot tea with extra sugar. I remembered reading that hot, sweet tea helped pregnant women with headaches. I wasn't pregnant but decided to try it, regardless.

I drank the tea and wrote my thoughts in the journal. After half an hour, I started to feel better until two Americans walked in. I thought it would be nice to meet fellow compatriots, but I thought wrong.

Their loud talking and random outbursts of laughter caused pulses of pain in my head. They didn't look my way and I didn't bother saying hello. I just hoped they'd finish whatever they were doing and leave. The owner, my savior, came in and led them out.

Writing in my journal served as a log and a way to get my thoughts together. Although I often didn't enjoy writing, I knew this to be important. When I was home and bored, I often opened up my past travel journals and surprised myself at what I'd done.

Some moments made me smile, while others stupefy me with the foolish actions I'd made. At that time, they seemed to make perfect sense, but looking back on it later, showed thoughtlessness. A lesson learned.

~*~*~

After an hour, I finished my writing and stepped outside to get some fresh air. There I met Filip and Agata, the Polish couple.

"Hi, you two. Where are you headed this late?"

"Hi, Aleksey. You see that building in the distance?" Filip pointed. "It's a small rescue post. In half an hour, there will be a free lecture about altitude sickness. Join us."

I thanked them and followed. We approached a small one-story building, with a large red cross by the door. When we entered, a young man greeted us. He guided us to sit at any of the available chairs facing a white board at the front.

The talk started on time. I looked around and counted ten people sitting beside me. One man and two women facilitated the class. They were volunteer doctors from England.

They talked about the available equipment at the facility. Most of it helped with altitude sickness. The small hospital even had a portable altitude chamber to help with more severe cases. Services were available, not only to trekkers, but also to Sherpa. Their lecture enlightened me, but the topic of altitude sickness interested me the most.

The young male doctor from England explained, "Altitude sickness has three forms. Mild altitude sickness is called "Acute Mountain Sickness" and is similar to a hangover. It causes headache, nausea and fatigue. This is very common.

"Some people are only slightly affected, while others feel awful. However, if you have AMS, you should take this as a warning sign that you are at risk for the more serious forms of altitude sickness. They are *High-altitude Pulmonary Edema*" and *High-altitude Cerebral Edema*," in short, HAPE and HACE. Both can be fatal within hours."

The doctor continued enthusiastically, "HAPE is excess fluid in the lungs and causes breathlessness. It is never normal to feel breathless when you are resting, even on the summit of Everest. This should be taken as a sign that you have HAPE and may die soon. HAPE can also cause a fever and coughing up spit.

"HACE is the most severe and causes fluid to build up in the skull. It causes confusion, clumsiness and stumbling. The first signs may be uncharacteristic behavior such as laziness, excessive emotion or violence. Drowsiness and loss of consciousness occur shortly before death.

"If you notice signs for HAPE or HACE, immediately descend. Pressure bags and oxygen tanks can buy time. If you have medicine that contains *acetazolamide*, take it."

The doctor finished his piece, and a young female doctor replaced him. She continued, "Mountain Sickness usually does not affect people below twenty-five hundred meters, that's eighty-two hundred feet.

"On a different subject, at the end of this class, we will sell *Diamox*. This medicine helps the body adjust to higher elevation. There are no known side effects.

"Most of the money made from selling Diamox will go toward helping Sherpa. There are many Sherpa casualties due to their poor treatment. While the climbers sleep in lodges or tents, many Sherpa commonly sleep outside to save money.

"Many do not have proper sleeping bags and warm clothing. Yet, they still take on the difficult climbing assignments to support their families. We use the money to purchase equipment for them, or at the very least, make sure they sleep at a lodge and get proper food."

The female doctor finished, and the next female doctor took her place to continue. "This is the end of our lecture. Thank you all for attending. If any of you know doctors or nurses who might be interested in volunteering here for a season, please let them know to apply online.

"We will now take individual questions and offer our services. For one hundred rupees, a bit over one US dollar, we can test your oxygen level and heartbeat. Also, we will now sell Diamox."

I waited my turn in line to take the test.

The doctor looked at me and smiled. "Have a seat. This won't take long." She placed a finger clip heart rate monitor around my index finger and waited a moment. "Let's see. Your oxygen saturation level is at eighty-four percent and heartbeat is ninety-eight. The numbers are not ideal but are fine for this altitude. The cold does not help either."

Since she said it was fine, I didn't question the results. The idea of buying Diamox troubled me. I didn't wish to use drugs or oxygen tanks on this journey, but preparation proved essential. I decided to buy Diamox and keep it for emergencies only.

"I'll buy several packets of Diamox, please. What is the dosage? Anything I should worry about after taking it?" I wanted to know the details.

"Try to take one pill at least twelve hours before ascending higher, preferably one in the morning and one in the evening. If you wish to start today, I recommend taking a lower dosage. One pill a day is enough. You can break it in half and take it twice a day.

"It really is a wonder drug for altitude sickness. But take it before you climb higher. Although the pill will work even after you get sick, the effects are greatly reduced and may not work in time." The female doctor slowly enunciated the last part.

After purchasing Diamox, I left the rescue post and walked back to my lodge. New information made me reevaluate the severity of altitude, but it did not change my choice on going alone. Hiring a guide would ruin the trip for me, and taking the medicine felt like cheating. I decided to push on as I always did, alone.

Back at the lodge, I ate a few snacks and went to sleep, ending another interesting day.

Chapter 16

In the morning, I considered staying an extra night to help acclimatize but decided against it. I would spend two nights at the next stop.

The road greeted me with a clear blue sky and crisp cold air. I took my time and climbed slowly. By now the trees were gone, replaced by broken stones and solitary boulders.

Gone were the green, lush colors, now replaced by the grey mountains, dried brown grass covered in snow and the blues of an occasional glacier.

Some clouds were high in the sky, as far as the eye could see, while others hovered around the tops of the pointy peaks. Eventually, the winds blew the grey mist onto the trail and obstructed my view of the beautiful high-altitude scenery.

As I approached Gokyo Point, several small lakes greeted me. I imagined water would be frozen in this frigid weather, but they weren't. I walked closer and tested the temperature. The water felt extremely cold. Why didn't it freeze?

The color of the water almost matched the sky, clear blue, but I could not see the bottom, even by the shore. It made me wonder, would I find fish here?

Gokyo Point had numerous buildings that were larger than previous settlements. Although there were several lodges available, only one had solar panels. I needed to recharge my phone.

Inside, a young man greeted me in English and showed me to my room. He also stressed the price of charging electronics. An hour of charging cost three hundred and fifty rupees, about four dollars. I paid for two hours. Music played an important role in my life.

I spent my afternoon and evening sitting in the common area next to the hot stove. Large windows surrounded me on all sides. The light of the setting sun saturated the scenery in its rich, orange color.

The sunset inspired me to write my thoughts in detail. At the same time, I listened to my new, favorite song, "Draw Your Swords," by *Angus* and *Julia Stone*. The Australian Indie pop singer, Angus Stone, sang it with such emotion, he inspired me to hum along. "Youuuu aaaare ... the only one." I didn't mind the weird look the young Nepalese man at the kitchen gave me.

Another day had ended and a new one would soon begin.

Chapter 17

At sunrise, I awoke with an urgent need. I tried to suppress it but realized it could not be ignored. The cold morning air no longer discouraged me from jumping out of bed and running directly to the bathroom.

As I opened the door, the impending pressure within me felt overwhelming. The sharp pain in my abdomen felt foreboding. I pulled down my pants in such a hurry, I almost slipped on the yellow ice around the squat toilet.

The light from outside had barely penetrated the frozen window and offered limited visibility. For a moment, I stood there and looked at the dark, ominous hole in the floor. I felt the cold air being sucked into it, like a vacuum. I immediately thought of a black hole, mysterious.

My stomach protested with loud sounds and brought me back to reality. I persevered and carefully approached the toilet. I thought of the serious complications of falling, to be so close, yet so far. It scared me, but this toilet would not get the better of me.

I got in the right position and started to relax. Immediately after, the sounds confirmed my ominous feeling. I had diarrhea.

After the unpleasant bathroom experience, I returned to my cold room exhausted. I took two tablets of my grandmother's diarrhea medicine and lay back in bed. Thankfully, the squat toilet was indoors. It made me recall a different name for squat toilets used in England, "the squatty potty."

Hunger made me get out of bed a few hours later. I put on warm clothing, which included my hat, and went to eat breakfast. My sore throat forced me to select garlic soup. I believed the only reason I had not gotten sick yet was because of this local dish.

The joy of doing nothing pleased me. I worked very hard at doing nothing, as I sat in one of the chairs and only moved my thumb to press the "next" button for a different song on my phone.

Late afternoon, I felt more energetic and decided to follow the "climb high, sleep low" concept. I stepped out and walked towards Gokyo Ri. Its height stood at almost fifty-four hundred meters, over seventeen thousand seven hundred feet, the tallest climb near Gokyo.

As I followed a dim trail, the climb offered a different kind of challenge. I no longer suffered with pain in my legs or headaches but from shortness of breath and lack of energy. About an hour into my climb, halfway, I had doubts of reaching the summit.

Every five to seven steps I needed to stop and catch my breath. It felt like I had run several marathons continuously. Breathing hard hadn't felt tedious because all I thought of was whether or not I could catch my breath.

The other problem was lack of energy. Every muscle in my body felt as soft as cotton. I couldn't muster up the strength to toughen them up. I could only lift my legs and move forward slowly.

After another hour, I finally saw the summit, marked by Tibetan prayer flags. At the same time, I saw movement of the only other people ahead of me, descending from a different side of the mountain.

I heard shouts but couldn't understand their words. Then I saw two Sherpas carrying a man. He wasn't moving. The panicked yells between the two Sherpas confirmed the man's poor condition. I guessed he hadn't reached the top.

Despite many breaks and the occasional thoughts of Mountain Sickness, I pushed onward. I no longer had any desire to turn back. Although there would be no one to carry me down, I had full confidence in myself.

After countless, breathless struggles, I reached the top. Without caring for the scenery, I first found a comfortable rock, and then sat down to admire the breathtaking reward.

The best artist couldn't replicate the beauty in front of me. Despite the many, symbolic pyramid-shaped mountains in all directions, Mount Everest outshined the rest. Although the closer mountains appeared similar and stood taller, the moment I set my eyes on Mount Everest, I knew it to be the one. Its peak glowed golden as if it were on fire.

As the sun slowly set behind me, a dark shadow climbed Mount Everest. Like a monster, it crept up and ate the daylight wantonly. However, it only made the phenomenon in front of me more spectacular.

The smaller the shine on the peak became, the deeper the colors glowed. I now understood the pictures where I'd seen the peak of a mountain replaced by a deity shining as brightly as if it were the sun.

I took out my camera and photographed away. I doubted I'd see something like this again.

After a while, I no longer looked at the sunset but at the mountains around me. All it took was a different angle and my outlook changed. I was no longer an admirer, or a bystander but a participant in my own story. A sense of accomplishment infused me.

While the light still shone, I tried to plan my climb for tomorrow, and what I saw shocked me. On one side lay the sky blue Gokyo Lakes that I passed the previous day. On the other side were steep mountains, similar to Gokyo Ri. Tomorrow I had to cross what lay between the two, a glacier.

I had never seen anything like this before, not in photographs, nor in my imagination. There lay what appeared to be a frozen river with ten to twenty-foot waves. It seemed as though the bottom of the mountain had been sliced open by a sharp blade, bringing out the moist insides, forever petrified in that state.

The beauty of the pale-blue colors made the glacier seem majestic. To think I had to cross this tomorrow excited me. Such unique lands were so unlike my home in Florida.

After a good rest, the climb down didn't pose a problem. I only took one break before reaching the lodge. The comfortable chair greeted me with open arms. I didn't even take my hat off. I simply sat there, immobile.

~*~*~

Evening approached. Several other climbers filled up the dining room. At that moment, I knew I had to move my body otherwise people might think something was wrong with me. I considered doing my laundry, but my wool unmentionables were odor resistant and persuaded me not to wash them.

I looked up and saw Filip and Agata enter the room. I waved my hand to have them join me. Agata seemed to be the same as always, energetic. Filip, on the other hand, had red eyes, a runny nose and had already sneezed several times before reaching me.

"You don't look so good there, buddy. What happened?" I asked.

"Oh, I think I am getting a cold. I thought it would go away during the day, but it has gotten worse. That altitude meeting was amazing. What did you think of it?"

I thought back on it. "It was eye opening. It made me realize how I lacked information and the severity of altitude. You remember the volunteer spots they talked about? Some of my friends would definitely be interested. Could you imagine spending several months here enjoying this beautiful scenery? If I were a doctor, I'd go."

Agata laughed. "I already know several of my girlfriends would gladly volunteer here. I know I would."

"Hey, did you two see the communist flags hanging in some of the villages? Are they doing this as a joke or are they serious? I don't get it." I grimaced.

Filip finally smiled. "Oh yeah, The *Communist Party* of Nepal is serious. They've been around since the nineteen fifties and have a strong presence in the government. All those flags you see along the way are their supporters. You were born in the USSR. You should know this much."

"Well, darn. I really had no idea. Good thing I didn't say any silly jokes that came to mind when I saw the flags. I don't keep up with the latest communist changes. As I see it, I'm an American."

"Agata and I have always wanted to visit Russia. For whatever reason, it never happened. Don't get me wrong, I'm not a supporter of communism. We are the opposite. Agata and I want to go to Moscow and join the protesters to support the revolution, to support the change for democracy. We have already done this in several countries. It's fun and we meet interesting people this way. Want to join us?"

Filip's question took me by surprised. "Me? I support democracy, but I've never protested like that. I support positive changes, but I try to do it one person at a time. I converse with strangers, get to know them and we share our views. Often my point gets across, and it makes people think. I believe it ignites an intellectual spark. Once an idea takes root in one's mind, it's tough to get rid of it. I might even write a small article about the subject on my website. Those that seek change will have no problem finding it. But hey, I have never done street protesting. If I'm in the area, I'll join you two."

Filip had an excited look on this face. "Definitely join us. I agree with what you said, but protesting together with the people is more intimate. After the event, we often get together with the locals and celebrate. We eat, drink and socialize. It's a great way to get to know them and make new friends. Standing up together for the same cause feels like brotherhood."

I smiled. "You're really passionate about this. When you come to the United States, let me know. You two are always welcome to stay at my home in Florida. I'll show you around and see if we can find some local protesting to do."

Agata laughed, "Thank you, Aleksey. That's very sweet of you. We'll make sure to keep in touch."

"Definitely keep in touch," Filip added.

"I saw you listening to music before. What music do you listen to? Is it Russian or English?" Agata asked.

"I listen to everything, Russian, English and others. Music is a lifesaver when I need an extra energy boost for climbing or to help me relax before bed. Did you know that personal music is banned in many marathons in the United States? Listening to music is considered doping, and supposedly, fast-paced music helps some runners run faster. Sometimes I almost feel guilty listening to it while climbing, almost. I won't be taking any altitude medicine or using oxygen tanks, though. Therefore, that should even things out. That's my excuse anyway."

I saw Filip's surprised expression. "Are you serious? Wow. United States sure is weird like that. It makes sense, though. I only use my phone to make calls. That's all."

"You two actually get phone reception here? Well, I wouldn't know. My phone is always on airplane mode to conserve battery power, and I don't buy local *SIM cards* for service. When I'm on my adventures, the only way to reach me is by email. This way I don't need to worry about home and I can completely disconnect. Although, the poker game on my phone comes in handy during long waits in line."

Agata looked outside the window. "Hey you two, look at this. I've never seen anything like it."

I looked outside and couldn't figure out what I saw. "It looks like smoke, but why is it on top of the lake? Is the smoke coming from the mountain next to it?"

All of a sudden, a ray of setting sun penetrated through the dark clouds and descended upon the water. It appeared as though a laser had burst onto the lake, setting it on fire.

Then a second and a third smaller ray passed through the clouds and landed on different parts of the water. Wherever they hit, thick mist developed immediately. As the clouds moved, the rays fell on the lake like the light of heaven penetrating the darkness. Strong winds blew and moved the mist toward the mountain. As the mist collected, it became a thick cloud rapidly ascending.

People gathered by the large windows and watched this amazing phenomenon. Before long, the sun had completely hidden behind the clouds and ended the show. For the next several seconds, no one said a word. I had been fortunate to witness this in person.

I broke the silence. "Well, this is not something I see every day. I wondered why the water didn't freeze. I guess the temperature is just right and that even the slightest change in temperature causes evaporation. But no matter how I explain it, words are not enough. I'm glad to have seen this."

Agata sat back down. "Me too. It's getting late, let's order dinner. I'm hungry."

The menu options didn't appeal to me. I frowned at the thought of eating more rice and beans and looked up in exasperation. Then behold, I saw a sign, written in English: "SALE! Roast Chicken with Fries! Only 750 Rupees!"

I couldn't remember the last time I ate meat. The very thought of eating chicken made my hands tremble with excitement and my mouth salivate. Even on sale, this would cost nine dollars, but I didn't care.

"That chicken on sale," I pointed at the sign, "I'm getting it. It's so expensive, though. I could get three plates of rice and beans for that."

Filip looked at me, "Like the rest of the items here, they all have been carried up by locals. Most do not have the luxury of using a horse or a donkey. They carry hundreds of pounds of food and equipment on their backs. The closer we get to the Base Camp, the more expensive it'll get."

I nodded. "Yeah, I understand, but I can't suppress the urge of eating meat. It's like every cell in my body craves it. I'm on a tight budget, but I'll economize later. Tonight, I'll treat myself."

We ordered. Soon my chicken arrived. I savored every piece and chewed the bones until I could not bite any further. The fatty oil dripped off the fries and excited me more than any gourmet meal I could think of.

Piece by piece the fries disappeared. I even broke them into several parts, opened my mouth and threw in a small piece at a time. This way I savored the salty flavor a bit longer.

Agata and Filip stared at me and chuckled, but I didn't care. Hunger truly was the best spice. Few times in my life had I enjoyed a meal to such an extent, and it only cost nine dollars.

~*~*~

After dinner, I said goodbye to the Polish couple and went to my room. It was dark, but a candle and matches were conveniently placed by the window. I lit the candle, moved towards the bed and then felt a sharp pain around my nose.

I took out my phone and recorded a video of myself. My nose looked red and scarred from dryness, with peeling skin around it. I took off the hat I'd worn even during sleep and observed my ruffled, dirty hair. It didn't move as I shook my head.

I looked at myself and shuddered. The deep purple spots under my eyes stood out. What has this trip done to me? I put the phone down and noticed my sunburnt, dry hands. The skin formed circular lines at the back of my hands that resembled scales. Will my skin look like this as I get older? A glance at the harsh future depressed me.

If I didn't do these kinds of trips, my skin would be unblemished, and my knees would not hurt from the abuse I've put them through. I wouldn't have to visit the doctor after every such journey. I wouldn't have to watch my body rapidly break down, one part at a time. Was it all worth it?

The moment this question crossed my mind, the depression cleared. A jolt of strength passed through me. These scars were my badges. What's a clean and beautiful body with nothing to remember it by but smooth skin and a routine smile? I shall wear my scars to remind myself and others that I'd been here. That I'd experienced life.

My scars will be my stories. My smile will be my pride. The smile that persevered through it all and that I was rewarded with living life to the fullest. I'd had many regrets, but no more. I had to finish this journey. I would make it to Mount Everest and climb as far as I could. There was no giving up. I could only go forward now. Doing what I dreamed of doing since I was a child, fulfilling my dreams, one at a time.

Chapter 18

I opened my eyes, breathing hard through the mouth. The congestion caused my nose to itch and hurt. I reached out to scratch. My fingers felt around the nostril and probed at the crust blocking the passage. I picked away at it and immediately felt warm liquid flow down.

I sat up. My head ached. The beam of light from my phone illuminated my fingers. They were bloody. My nostrils must have gotten too dry and caused the skin to crack. I cleaned my face and tried to sleep. I needed the strength for tomorrow's climb.

As the sun rose, I packed and then departed. The lodge family informed me of a sacred lake in the opposite direction of where I needed to go. There was no trail leading to it. Instead, they gave me simple instructions directing me north out of Gokyo. I thought of visiting it but changed my mind. I needed to keep moving forward.

The brown patches of dried up grass and dirt mixed with stones surrounded me, but it wasn't long before I hiked over a hill, and the glacier I studied yesterday appeared before me. The blue and silver colors almost blinded me. I put on sunglasses and studied the best route down.

With enthusiasm, I ventured forward. The climb down felt easy. Crushed rocks littered the glacier and offered little stability, but I didn't become complacent. When I used my foot to scatter the debris, clear blue ice glistened back at me.

At that moment, I realized I walked on a large sheet of ice covered by a layer of ground up rocks. I considered putting on crampons for safety. The metallic spikes fixed to the bottom of boots were for stability. Laziness won again. I decided against it.

Solitary boulders, several stories high, stood tall and surrounded me. They were not made of stone but large chunks of ice. It seemed as if they policed the area. If I misbehaved, they might just step on me to maintain the serenity.

The map confirmed this to be the Ngolumba Glacier. The farther I went, the more mysterious the environment became. There were no trails, signs, or markings of any kind. I made my own route and tried to make it to the other side using the safest and most intriguing way.

Occasionally, I saw clean patches of ice exposed for the world to see, with not a speckle of dust. I guessed nature liked to be clean sometimes. It also reminded me to be careful and not slip. The crampons had been placed deep in my backpack, and the very thought of digging for them antagonized me.

After an hour and a half, my energy level dropped significantly, and I concentrated on making my way out of the valley instead of exploring the area further. Yesterday it appeared to be a simple challenge to cross the glacier looking down from Gokyo Peak, but as I walked, it felt like a maze.

After what seemed like hours, I climbed a steep, icy hill. I huffed and puffed and slipped a few times until I reached the end and noticed an unnaturally straight dirt line separating the two different ecosystems, silver to my side, dark brown ahead.

Nature fascinated me. Science tried to explain the logic behind the workings of nature but failed to describe the enchanting beauty behind it. I only started to respect and protect the environment after experiencing it firsthand. Simply reading about it in my youth had not inspired me to respect nature.

When I stepped back onto the hard, dirt surface, I used a map and compass to coordinate my position to plan my course. It wasn't difficult. With the clearly visible Gokyo Ri Peak on one side and Mount Everest on the other, I knew where to go. If I got lost, well, there would be a grand adventure awaiting me, a win-win situation. Getting lost seemed just as exciting as digging for treasure when I was a kid.

Another hour passed and I saw the settlement of Dragnag. It stood at the height of forty-seven hundred meters, about fifteen and a half thousand feet and consisted of six, small one-story houses. Three were attached and made a long row of windows. The gray, blue and green colored roofs were the only way to tell the different houses apart. Other than that, there was nothing unique about Dragnag. I liked the green roof and decided to stay at that lodge for the night.

I knocked and an older Nepalese woman opened the door. She had a confused look on her face. Like, what was I doing here?

I smiled and waved my hand. "Hi. Room. One night. Sleep?" With my hands together next to my right ear, I indicated a sleeping position.

The look of understanding flashed on her face. She stepped aside and waved me in.

The room she led me to had a bed and a window. It was more than I expected. *"Yo kati ho?"* I rubbed my two fingers together denoting the universal sign for money. She replied in Nepali, but I couldn't understand her. I handed her a pen and a piece of paper.

She wrote an agreeable number, and I verbally accepted. I then pointed at my watch and opened my mouth, chewing imaginary food. My hand held an imaginary spoon. She understood what I wanted and wrote the time for dinner. I didn't ask about the type of food. I didn't think the menu would stray far from the staple rice and beans, with maybe soup on the side.

I unpacked and went outside the lodge to wash my unmentionables. Washing anything else would be too large to dry in time and might end up frozen. After two hours, I finished my chores and went to the kitchen to eat dinner. Not to my surprise, I was the only person staying overnight.

The hostess called out to a girl about eleven years old. She served me a dish of garlic soup and fried rice with veggies. I devoured the fried rice and enjoyed the spicy garlic soup. It was so strong, I thought my tongue would melt, but it didn't stop me from finishing the entire bowl.

After the meal, I wrote a few sentences in my journal and went to bed in the same clothes I wore during the day. The dirt on the heavy blankets over my sleeping bag showed I wasn't the only person to do so. As I closed my eyes, I shivered one last time from the cold before falling sleep.

Chapter 19

When I awoke, I immediately felt nauseated and reached for the phone to checked the time. The bright screen showed ten forty-seven at night. The bed felt warm, and I didn't want to get up. If I lay still, maybe the queasiness would go away. If I could keep myself from throwing up, it might pass.

Couldn't I just have one peaceful night's rest without something happening? I closed my eyes and tried to fall asleep. My stomach grumbled and my mouth salivated. I tightened the sleeping bag around me. Damn it. If I didn't get up, I knew I'd vomit on my equipment and clothing.

Slowly, I unzipped my bag and sat up. At that moment, a wave of nausea reached a new height. I couldn't hold it in any longer and quickly pushed the bag away, then ran for the door. There was only a second or two left.

The door of my room slammed open, and I immediately went to the end of the hallway. I entered the bathroom and got on my knees. Warm liquid burst from my mouth and into the white, ceramic squat toilet. My abdomen hardened to the point of pain. My eyes watered. I vomited again and again.

I thought it would never end but eventually it did. I gasped for air. Both of my hands were on the sides of the toilet. Moonlight from the window illuminated the contents of my dinner. I clearly saw the undigested pieces of fried rice and veggies. Normally, such a view looked unsightly, but now I didn't care. The pain in my stomach made me ignore everything else.

After the ache subsided, I looked to my left and saw a wooden bucket. I wanted to wash my face. I pulled at the ladle, but it didn't budge. The water in the bucket was frozen solid.

I reached for the wall, stood up slowly and went back to the room to get my private stash of toilet paper. I cleaned up and lay back down to warm up. The momentary peace didn't last long. Another wave of nausea hit, and I ran back to the bathroom.

For the next hour, I crouched over the toilet purging my dinner, then lunch and surprisingly, breakfast. I thought it had already digested, but the small, undigested pieces of pasta were clearly visible. The human body amazed me.

I barely stood up. My body shook violently from weakness and abuse. I considered drinking a small amount of water to re-hydrate and went to the kitchen.

The older woman stood by the entrance and looked at me. I considered asking her for assistance and medicine, but after seeing her expression, I knew she wouldn't be useful. Her eyes showed fear and apprehension.

"*Tato pani*," I asked for hot water. She seemed to understand and nodded.

After fifteen minutes, she placed a thermos with hot water and a clean cup on the table next to me. She then quickly re-treated to her room and slammed the door shut. I guessed she worried about catching the stomach flu. I didn't blame her. It was only natural.

I poured a small amount of water into the cup and placed my shaking hands around it to feel the warmth. Before the water cooled, I ran back to the toilet and continued to vomit.

For the next three hours, I suffered countless episodes like this. At the end, I could no longer run back and forth and sat next to the toilet. Every time I tried to stand upright, sharp pains in my abdomen forced me to bend like a shrimp. There-fore, I just sat there and didn't move. My body trembled uncon-trollably. The filthy clothing I wore didn't concern me in the least. I only wanted to feel better.

After four hours, I felt relief with my bowel completely emptied. No matter how my body tried, nothing came out. I used the support of the walls to stand up. I looked like the *Hunchback of Notre-Dame*, with my body bent to almost ninety degrees as I slowly walked to my room. I crawled into the sleep-ing bag, placed two additional blankets over me and closed my eyes.

~*~*~

As I lay in bed, my stomach grumbled, ached and demanded sustenance, but the very thought of food made me feel nauseated. I now understood how people withered away from starvation in hospital beds. It wasn't their lack of desire, they simply couldn't eat.

My phone displayed eleven in the morning. It didn't seem like I would be going anywhere today. The last several hours showed slight improvement, but I was in no condition for strenuous activity.

In the afternoon, I went to the kitchen. The stove made it the warmest room in the house. I sat on one of the available chairs. The owner came by to check on me. She didn't say a word, but her presence felt reassuring.

I sipped warm, black tea and contemplated my thoughts on paper. The abundance of time gave me the opportunity to write this fascinating experience in detail.

If all went well, in three to four days, I'd be at the Everest Base Camp. My plan to fatten up failed miserably. No amount of rice and beans helped. As for that darn chicken sale a few days ago, that wasn't the first time I'd fallen for such a trick. Meat for sale in a remote mountain camp. What was I thinking?

Any food for sale here spelled trouble and should have been a definite warning sign. The kitchen probably tried to get rid of the chicken before it completely spoiled. Gluttony had gotten the better of me. I admit though, it tasted heavenly, and the nine dollars also included this very memorable night.

When I return home and sit comfortably in my room, I'd look back on this and laugh. "Ha!" I'd say. "That was so stupid!"

Thoughts of home made me feel nostalgic. I missed my computer. Video games didn't interest me as much anymore, but I always replayed the same game since high school, *Baldur's Gate*. It's a role-playing game where my character roamed the vast virtual world.

There wasn't a definite choice of good or evil but a series of countless options which made up the story. Despite this, I tried to stay true to my character, literally and virtually, and leaned towards the hero alignment.

Being a bad guy seemed too boring. All they wanted was to kill and destroy. What's the fun in that? I planned to replay this game upon return. It didn't matter that I'd get bored with it in a day or two.

I missed cooking and eating. When I finished exploring Nepal and go to China, I'd eat everything I wanted. I'd get pizza, steak, ice cream and lots of sweets. I'd listen to music without the worry of battery life. I'd finally take a shower and breathe fresh air without difficulty. Oh, how sweet the air would be.

The thought of effortless breathing brought joy. I only now realized the importance of simple little things. Like the famous line in many of the sad romantic songs, "You don't know what you got till it's gone."

As I wrote in my journal, the hostess looked at me from time to time and threw a log into the stove. It warmed me up every time.

The thoughts of adventure confused me. What defined an adventurer? Was I one? What did it cost me going through pain, cold and many discomforts for the sake of the moment? To say that I'd done it? Why am I here? For the pleasure or liking? To find the answers, I first had to make these memories, then look back and reflect on what I'd done in comparison to my other experiences.

Despite the desire to be home at this very moment and indulge myself in its comforts, the pleasures of home wouldn't last. After several days, I'd be bored again and crave a new adventure. Maybe that's why I liked the road so much, it always changed.

Lost in my thoughts, I suddenly realized the evening arrived. All these ideas and the countless strokes of the pen worked up a mighty appetite. My stomach grumbled and demanded food. I tried a bowl of noodle soup. Along with it, I swallowed my grandma's stomach medicine.

The food held, and I planned to leave in the morning. Tomorrow would be a difficult day. I had to climb Cho La Pass.

According to the map, it lay at the height of almost fifty-seven hundred meters, a bit over seventeen thousand feet.

Chapter 20

Morning came too soon. I stared at my porridge thoughtfully. Once I departed, there would be no toilets. Large boulders would have to do. After much consideration, I decided to eat the porridge. I needed the energy.

I gave the hostess cash for my stay and walked towards the exit.

"Hey," a familiar voice called out.

I turned around and saw the hostess with a worried expression. She approached and handed me two ketchup-sized packets.

"Energy." She pointed upward with her finger.

I looked at the packets and realized they were energy boost gels. I smiled. "Thank you."

The woman nodded and walked me to the door.

It only took several minutes to leave this small settlement. I then followed a dim trail. Small rocks crunched beneath my feet. There were no trees or vegetation in sight, just large rock, glaciers and snow-capped mountains. I steadied my pace to conserve energy.

Within an hour, the trail disappeared and a harsh ascent greeted me, with different sized boulders that blocked my path. I knew this to be the start of Cho La Pass.

Half an hour had passed and I was ready to pitch my tent and call it a day. Breathing had never been so difficult. A miniscule number of three to six steps forced me to stop. Every breath of air only increased the desire for more. I felt like a fish out of water slowly drowning in oxygen.

The sheer cold forced me to cover my face with a wool scarf. This hindered my breathing further. However, breathing without it felt too cold.

Boulders three stories high blocked my way. I placed my hands and feet in various crevices and climbed further. I didn't bother using rope to secure myself and practiced my climbing skills. The last few feet were always the most difficult as the heavy backpack sapped my stamina.

After climbing several boulders, I ate the two energy gel packets and took out a bottle of water. Nothing came out. The water was frozen. Adding salt and sugar to the water didn't help much. I placed the aluminum bottle in the inner pocket of my jacket to warm it up.

I tried to move faster to keep up my body temperature. The rays of the sun beamed behind the Pass. Once I'd reach the top, I hoped to be warm again. Climbing in the shadow only dimmed my mood further.

The slightest motion forward felt like a mile run. Cold sweat ran down my back. The backpack had never felt this heavy. I occasionally chewed on a piece of candy and discarded the wrappers to lessen the weight. Yes, I dirtied this holy mountain. Yes, I felt guilty, but at the moment I didn't care.

People who comfortably sat home and judged climbers for trashing the mountains have not experienced its difficulties. Most have not gone through the tribulations of the mountain. Even a simple candy wrapper felt like a heavy dumbbell, weighing me down until I couldn't move farther.

I promised myself to donate money to a Mount Everest cleanup agency when I returned home. It would be the least I could do.

As I climbed up the mountain, I chanted aloud the same phrase like a possessed soul. "One step at a time."

Occasionally I looked up and thought I saw the summit of Cho La Pass. When I reached it, there would always be more to climb. The mountain played tricks on me. It hid the final destination and tried to break down my will with false hope and illusions, but I didn't give up. I stopped looking up and kept pushing forward. Having expectations led to disappointments. Knowing the finish line didn't help.

My stomach grumbled. I felt hungry, yet nauseated. I knew my body was famished.

After another hour passed, I entered the state of acceptance. I got used to the aches and pains. The distance didn't matter. I simplified my goal to a single step, and then another, endlessly pushing forward.

After countless, breathless struggles, the end seemed near, maybe another two hundred feet. With every stolen glance upward, my heartbeat quickened with excitement. I tried my best to calm down.

The mountain tortured me like a temptress, with promises of false hope and heartbreaks. It seduced me with its every curve and bend, making me go farther and farther. But as I climbed closer, my salvation, the sun, welcomed me with its gentle touch on my face. I knew there would no lies here as it held me in its warm embrace.

I finally reached the top of Cho La Pass and immediately looked for a comfortable rock to sit on. I took off my backpack and faced the view.

The mountains around me soared as if they wished to challenge the sky itself. They dominated the horizon in every direction I looked.

~*~*~

Despite the warming sun, sweaty clothing chilled me. I unpacked a dry jacket and put it on. Feeling warmer, I looked ahead and admired the blue color of the glacier. It reminded me of frosting on a cake, smooth, shiny and delicious. I wanted to lick it, but that would be a bad idea. Instead, I drank a few gulps of the melted water from my canteen.

Crampons would be necessary to cross this glacier. Otherwise, I'd slide down off the mountain. I laughed just thinking about it.

In the distance, I saw a group of four climbers slowly moving down. It looked like two Sherpas and a young couple. The sight of them comforted me. It seemed I had climbed the right mountain.

The batteries in my camera lost power. I kept forgetting that cold slowed their chemical reaction. Despite the fact that batteries are better preserved in the cold, it also made them useless until warmed. I had to remove the camera batteries and warm them up in my hands.

The rock I sat on felt like the most comfortable chair in the world, with a panoramic view of mountains as a bonus. This time I collected the candy wrappers and placed them in my pocket. The descent would not be as difficult. I didn't worry about the extra weight.

After half an hour of rest, I judged my body fit enough to continue. I affixed crampons and looked for the best way to climb down to the glacier. Several visible footprints made by previous climbers offered options. Not using rope to secure myself, I climbed down the summit of Cho La Pass to the ice below. The distance didn't seem far.

When I made it down to the flat surface of the glacier, I felt the spikes of the crampons sink into the ice. I moved forward with confidence. It took half an hour to cross the glacier until I reached the hard surface of rock again. I unclipped the crampons and trekked downhill.

I disliked the descent. Although I used less energy, it felt tedious using different muscles. In addition, the downhill increased the pressure on my knees, up to six times, and the heavy backpack didn't help. Correct posture of leaning forward benefited, but it was difficult to maintain.

Eventually I descended Cho La Pass and saw the settlement of Dzangola. I looked around and didn't see a single tree. Brown soil, crushed rocks and boulders encompassed everything.

When I looked up, it seemed as though the white mountaintops taunted me, and asked, "Who is that puny thing down there?"

Nothing stood out about the small settlement. It had six, one-story houses. The only cheerful parts were the different colored roofs, four green, one gray and a stunning red. I chose my favorite color green.

A young Nepalese man greeted me at the door and arranged my room. I wasn't very talkative and went directly to sleep. A case of diarrhea woke me up within an hour.

Soon after, I went to the kitchen and ordered potato soup.

The young man by the stove frowned. "You need to eat more. This little soup is not enough."

I smiled. "OK. I'll order a second bowl of potato soup. I can't eat hard food. My stomach hurts." I rubbed my belly.

He nodded and poured a second bowl. I noticed he added an extra piece of potato. How nice of him.

As I ate my meal, I felt discouraged having missed one day of the climb due to stomach flu. I felt troubled, slow and delayed, as if I missed something important and needed to catch up.

After dinner, I eased myself into the sleeping bag and passed out immediately.

Sometime during the night, I awoke from the loud noises outside. I looked out the window and saw a group of Nepalese men and women next to a bonfire. They danced and sang in their native tongue.

I toyed with the idea of going down to join them, but it felt like too much effort. Earplugs did the job to dampen the noise. Sweet dreams followed.

Chapter 21

Missing the one day did not sit well with me. In the morning, I decided to climb two days' worth of distance and make it to Gorakshep by nightfall. My map showed it to be the very last available settlement before Mount Everest.

As I made my way to Lobuche, my original settlement destination, the trail seemed less and less distinct. Most of the climb ventured through a valley, with mountains on all sides.

Often there were forks in the valleys. Those were my nemesis. Back home the romance of taking the road less traveled seemed so inspiring. Now that I had limited time, resources and energy, I just wanted to find the fastest and less calorie-consuming route. I promised myself, for the journey in China, I'd take the path less traveled.

Two times, I lost my way and had to backtrack. Taking the same route back felt like a chore, less for the caloric loss, but more because I had to persevere through the same mountain scenery again. It felt less stimulating, less inspiring. Like reusing an ice cream waffle cone, the crunchiness was gone if used the second time around.

After several hours, I made it to Lobuche and then pushed on ahead. Three glaciers separated the way to Gorakshep, Khumbu Glacier being the largest. I made it to Gorakshep by afternoon despite losing my way multiple times.

Thoughts of food consumed me. I had to eat to restore my energy.

~*~*~

Gorakshep had a cluster of buildings. It was the largest settlement that I'd seen for the past several days. The structures seemed similar to one another and most were two-stories tall and adorned with various flags. The brickwork around the windows showed decorative patterns, which beautified the settlement. Mount Everest stood clearly behind these buildings.

Again, I picked the largest, green-roofed lodge to purchase a meal.

A young Nepalese man opened the door and spoke broken English. "What you want?"

When I heard him, I remembered my friend's favorite saying. "You'll get more with honey than vinegar."

I smiled. "Hi. Do you sell food?"

The young man looked at me for a moment. "In." He waved his hand with a serious expression. "Go there." He pointed. "Tell man in kitchen to give menu," and then he walked away.it

I followed the hallway to a large room. Two groups of foreigners sat at different tables, an older couple and two young men. I wanted company and decided to join them for lunch.

The two young men were busy playing cards. I approached the older couple.

"Hi, there. Can I join you two?" I tested their English.

"Of course, you can. Have a seat. We met several days ago at a different lodge," the older man stated.

I thought about it for a moment. "That's right. I remember now. Glad you two made it here safely. Where are you from? I can tell you have an American accent."

The woman spoke up, "That's right. We're from New Mexico. Are you from the States too?"

"Yep, I live in Florida. If not for Everest, I'd be at the beach swimming in the warm waters of the Atlantic Ocean right now." I sighed with longing. "I love New Mexico. Carlsbad Caverns is an amazing national park. You two are far from home. How are you faring in Nepal?"

The woman smiled. "Yes, New Mexico is beautiful. I wouldn't want to live anywhere else. It's incredibly scenic and diverse. We have mountains, deserts, snow and plenty of forests. Florida is nice too, but it's not New Mexico. I like Nepal. It's so beautiful, but Charles here caught a sinus infection."

Charles sniffled. "Oh, yeah. This sinus infection is keeping me from getting a good night's sleep. If only I brought more medicine. It's OK though, we're almost at the Base Camp."

I looked at Charles's red nose and watery eyes. "I've learned to carry extra medicine. If you want, I can give you enough Benadryl for the next several days. It doesn't have much effect on me. If it can help one of us, I'll be happy."

Charles' eyes glittered with hope, like a candle in a dark room. "Are you sure you'll have enough for yourself?"

The memory of having to pop out Benadryl from the four packets to place them into a smaller, self-made container still bored me to tears. "Definitely enough. I over packed on medicine. Let me give you some right now."

"Thank you. I might finally be able to get a good night's sleep. Hopefully, Jenny will get some sleep tonight too. She tells me my snoring is out of this world."

Jenny pinched his shoulder. "I didn't say that. I said I woke up a few times, that's all." She turned to look at me. "Thank you for the Benadryl. I'm sure it will help Charles. I'm Jenny. What's your name?"

"My name is Aleksey. It's nice to meet other Americans. Speaking simplified English to locals has degraded my vocabulary. It feels like I'll end up using short sentences and simple words when I return to the U.S."

Jenny nodded. "I fear the same will happen to us, too. Although we practiced Nepali before arriving, most locals speak enough English to want to practice with us, giving us little choice to use Nepali. Will you be staying here tonight?"

"I don't know, probably. I'll have lunch first, then climb Kalapathar Mountain. It's approximately five thousand six hundred meters, which is a bit over eighteen thousand feet for us Americans. I'm not sure how long it'll take me. If I make it back early enough, I'll eat and go toward the Base Camp to set up my tent there. I've really had no opportunity to use it yet. So disappointing."

Charles took a deep breath. "You brought your tent? Well done. Although I advise you to stay here tonight and leave at dawn tomorrow, but if you end up going, please be careful."

"So, what did you two order for lunch?"

Our conversation continued until the food arrived. After a solid meal of rice and beans, I left my backpack with one of the lodge workers and took the trail to Kalapathar.

~*~*~

I stood at the edge of Kalapathar Mountain and looked up until my neck hurt. There was no ice or snow. Not even at the top. Why was I doing this again? I hoped to get an answer at the summit.

A well-worn trail led the way. Despite the intense incline, there was no need to use climbing equipment. I dragged my feet with little motivation across the rocky terrain as the winds tried to push me down. The climb didn't seem worth the effort.

After half an hour, the trek felt even more difficult than Gokyo Peak. Halfway to the summit, I ran out of energy and considered crawling but that would dirty my clothing.

A few minutes later, I stood next to a boulder with one hand supporting myself. I couldn't figure out if I would vomit or not. In the end, I held it in and pushed on. I didn't want to lose my first solid meal.

Fifty feet before the summit, I only had the energy for two steps at a time. The anger and frustration welled within me. I used it as fuel to push farther and take that last step to reach the summit. "Damn it! You stupid mountain!" The winds slowed down for a moment and silence beckoned.

This momentary stillness forced me to look around in appreciation. "And . . . thank you."

I sat on a rock nearby and took in the view. Three peaks stood in front of me, aligned in a row from the lowest on the left to the highest on the right. I recognized Mount Everest to be the one in the middle. Yet again, it wasn't the tallest from my viewpoint.

Was the climb worth it? The Kalapathar Mountain wasn't, but now I had no regrets. My curiosity was sated. I did what I wanted.

My altimeter showed a bit over fifty-six hundred meters, or

around eighteen thousand five hundred feet. I remembered that at zero elevation, which is sea level, the oxygen is more compressed making it easier to breath. The higher I climbed the thinner the oxygen became.

I felt curious about the percentage of oxygen I breathed in and pulled up a chart that I'd saved previously on my phone. At the current height of fifty-six hundred meters, the oxygen level showed to be slightly over ten percent. My home in Florida, with no elevation, had twenty-one percent. I complimented my body on surviving in only half the usual amount.

The climb down didn't take long, and the round trip totaled a bit over two hours. I returned to the lodge and ordered dinner. I had no doubt I would reach the old Everest Base Camp tonight. The new Everest Base Camp is in a different location and would be too far.

The two young men still played their card game. I felt curious and approached.

"Hi. What are you two playing?"

The taller man, with long, blond hair and a thick beard, looked at me. "Don't know the name of the game, man, but it's fun. Want to play? It's better with three or four people."

"Great. You looked so excited playing the game, I wanted to join too. Is it hard to learn?"

"Nah. It's easy, man. Some Nepalese guy taught it to us a week ago. My friend and I can't stop playing it now. We decided to name it 'The Nepalese Guy' card game."

I loved their creativity. The game fascinated me. I wrote the rules in my journal.

~*~*~

After dinner, I collected my backpack and returned to the trail. According to the map, it should only be two hours to the old Everest Base Camp.

The first half hour of the trail felt easy to follow. Afterward, it slowly disappeared and large boulders with crushed rocks lay in the mix obscuring the way. I used the map and compass to direct my way. I didn't see a soul to ask for directions.

After an hour and a half, I finally saw a rectangular, plastic sign hung by ropes at the corners. It said "Everest Base Camp 2012." I approached and studied the different names written with a black marker.

I couldn't believe people carried markers with them this far just to leave their names here. Heck, I didn't even know there was a sign here. I had a pen but didn't bother using it. The sign would probably be replaced in a few months anyway.

The sun slowly changed to dark orange, and I needed to look for a good camping spot. A few minutes away from the sign, I found a flat area and set up my tent. It didn't take long.

When I finished, the sun had set and the last remaining light hovered over the horizon. I sat on a rock and wrote of the past day in my journal. Not long after, my eyes started to close despite all my effort to stay awake.

I entered the tent, slid into the sleeping bag with all of my clothing on and closed my eyes. The blackness came over me like a blanket. No thoughts interfered as my mind drifted.

~*~*~

After several hours, I awoke. The bag felt warm, but I put on boots and went out to pee. As I stood there, feeling the pressure lessen, I admired the half-moon. It shone and lit up the glacier ahead of me.

I loved the moon. In Roman mythology, the goddess of the moon was called Diana. She kept me company on all of my journeys. Even in the darkest of nights, she lighted the way.

Each time I exhaled I saw fog. My cheeks tingled, half-numb from the cold, but it didn't bother me. After I finished my business, I studied the surroundings.

I felt a sense of wonder, as though for the moment I stood on a different world, somewhere new and fascinating. Every time I turned my head, the ice glittered and resembled a kaleidoscope. The stars dazzled with such vibrancy, it felt as though a wave of light came together to wash away the darkness.

I found a flat rock and sat down. Some moments were perfect, just as they were. Nothing needed to be changed. Often, they appeared unexpectedly. I didn't fight them and simply appreciated the present.

It seemed the older I became, the fewer of these moments I experienced. The more I lived, the less fascinating everything became. Still nice, still pleasant, more stable, but the sense of wonder slowly disappeared, only to be revisited when I took the leap and tried something different.

After experiencing the mountains here, could others compare in the future? Would they bring out such strong emotions as now? Would standing atop the highest mountain make others insignificant? I hoped not.

As much as I hated comparisons, somehow my mind compared without permission and subconsciously issued a ranking. If the rank were high, I'd be rewarded with a sense of wonder and enlightenment. If not, then it would just be another mountain scenery.

The more I experienced, the higher the bar rose. Reaching a new high was becoming more and more difficult. I sounded like an addict. Maybe I was. I just couldn't find a label for my addiction.

The rock I sat on froze my rear and I felt the chill creeping up. I stood and climbed back into my tent. The sleeping bag radiated warmth, as if to welcome me back. It would never be warm without me, and I couldn't be warm without it. Would I call this a symbiotic relationship?

The cold, fresh air had invigorated me. I no longer felt tired. Various thoughts raced through my mind. Like, mountain climbers had to poop, too. It's not something most people think about or even consider.

The act of braving the mountains elevated the climber beyond pooping. Climbers became almost like unicorns and princesses, who didn't poop. It was magic. But to share a little secret, we pooped. And no, we didn't dig holes in the ice to cover it up. It became another frozen part of the mountain. Maybe the growth of Mount Everest, four millimeters per year, was partly caused by this. I wondered.

The subject of climbers and bathrooms reminded me of astronauts. They stayed in spacesuits for hours, even days at a time? The spaceship lacked gravity and made it even more difficult to use the toilet. Wouldn't their deposits just float? How did they do it?

Thinking far back, I remembered from my past research that astronauts wore space diapers. Grown men and women, soldiers, the epitome of humanity, wore diapers. Was I disappointed? A little.

I didn't know why. Maybe I preferred ignorance, or even the unicorn concept, but not diapers. That was the harsh reality of life, I guessed. Similar complicated subjects kept me up for a while longer until sleep embraced me.

Chapter 22

Getting out of the sleeping bag in the morning felt like stepping into a cold shower. I unzipped the tent and went outside. The frigid air hit me like a sledgehammer. I immediately went back in and put on a second layer of clothing. The clear blue sky didn't help to offer warmth.

A breakfast of beef jerky, an energy bar and mixed nuts filled my belly. Packing up the tent felt like a chore, as if I were a child again and my mother reminded me to make my bed.

An hour passed before I had everything organized the way I wanted it. I believed that if I took care of my equipment, the equipment would take care of me. It also helped to preserve it better and saved me money.

I took a selfie with the Mount Everest sign, and then made my way across the Khumbu glacier to the new Everest Base Camp. The journey was not difficult, the terrain unchanged.

Along the way, I found a dim trail, or simply a convenient path leading ahead. As I hopped from rock to rock, I heard footsteps behind me and turned around. To my surprise, I saw a young Nepalese man. I waited for him to catch up.

The man didn't have a backpack, water or any equipment. He wore sufficient clothing but nothing else. I waved my hand. "Hi there. Where are you going?"

With hands in his pockets, he approached. "Hi. I'm going to the Base Camp. You too?" He spoke proficient English and looked to be in his early twenties.

"Yep. Let's keep moving and talk at the same time. Did you leave your equipment in Gorakshep?"

He walked next to me. "Yes. I'm here to scout the way for my group. Didn't think it would take so long. We shouldn't be too far. I hope no more than forty-five minutes."

"I hope so too. You're a guide? That's cool. Do you want some water?"

His eyes shone with excitement. "Yes, please." He took a bottle of water, opened it and tilted it back. The water poured into his mouth without the bottle touching his lips. After several mouthfuls, he closed the lid and passed it back. "Thank you."

"No problem. How big is your group?"

"Two people, an older couple. This is my vacation before I start college. I'm here to make some money as a guide before classes begin. I want to scout the trail to know the route. When I get back, I'll take them to the Base Camp, the end of their journey. We'll go back to Namche later."

He surprised me. Here I was, struggling with all of my effort to make it this far, and he was doing this as a part-time job in between semesters. This motivated me greatly. Not.

After a quick conversation, he rushed ahead to make better time.

~*~*~

It took less than an hour for me to reach the new Everest Base Camp. It wasn't much different from the old one, with colorful prayer flags hanging in one spot atop a pile of rocks. There was no snow. Only black rock mixed with ice and soil, which made a crunchy mix. Occasional spears of ice protruded from the surface.

I looked toward Mount Everest and saw a frozen cascade of white and blue flowing down like a painting. I'd seen this scenery in a photograph once before, which didn't compare to the real thing. Much of Khumbu glacier was brilliant white, but its deep crevasses were pure sapphire blue. Unimaginable, stunningly blue.

I stood there for a moment, admiring the cold beauty. It sent a chill through me that the warm rays of the sun could not thaw. Did I have to climb that?

I felt lost. I finally realized that I did not have a clear map directing me to the top of Mount Everest, nor the remotest idea of how to go about it. I glanced ahead and decided I'd go as far as I could and figure things out along the way.

With every step forward, I progressed toward the unknown. I had to go northeast, but that's all I knew. At least it wasn't *North by Northwest*. I laughed at the silly pun. It didn't matter because as long as I could go forward, I'd keep moving. I didn't worry nor over-complicate the situation with useless thoughts. A calm mind made the best decisions. Or so I hoped.

Two hours passed until I hit a dark, granite mountain wall. I didn't know if it was the right way but knew it to be Mount Everest. I now only needed to move forward, or, in this case, upward.

I studied the best climbing path that looked like a vertical staircase. I took out rope, *carabineers* and other climbing equipment. The easiest path showed a clearing approximately every twenty-five feet, with enough space to rest.

I tightened my backpack, secured the equipment and faced the mountain in front of me. My gloved hands felt the surface and reached for a good grip. With fingers locked in a small crevice, my left leg found support and jolted my body upright. My right arm released the first crevice and searched for a new one. Arms and legs worked in sequence, finding a good hold, one after the other, as I climbed higher and higher.

I didn't look down, only concentrated on the familiar pattern of climbing. My body was infused with energy. The higher I went the calmer and more confident I felt. The top of the first clearing, the next break, looked to be about six feet ahead.

I stretched high with my arm to get that perfect grip and felt something slowly slide out of the left pocket of my jacket. I glanced down, and my eyes widened. I took a deep breath and could only let out two simple words. "Damn it."

I watched my cellphone slide out of the unzipped pocket as gravity pulled at it.

The moment lasted no more than a second but felt like an eternity. Nothing could be done as I watched the phone slip away.

Clump. Clump. Clump.

I heard the sound of my phone hitting parts of Mount Everest and finally land at the very spot where I'd started.

My hands tightened the grip. I wanted to curse aloud. Different emotions surfaced as I stared at the dark rock in front of me. My lips closed tight and my breathing quickened as the anger rose in my throat, then erupted. "Dammit!" I yelled.

I held still for a moment and then relaxed. My right arm lowered as I looked for a grip to climb down. The descent reminded me of its difficulty. Climbing down took significantly more skill than climbing uphill.

Both of my legs hit the ground. My arms trembled, and I wasn't sure if fatigue or frustration had set in.

I looked down and glared at the phone next to my feet. If my glare had powers, it would have turned the phone to dust. If I hadn't needed it, I'd have stomped it to pieces. I wouldn't have left a single piece intact, but I needed it to listen to music.

I picked it up and stared. The phone looked to be in perfect condition, not a crack or a scratch on the screen. Only several spots of dirt were on the protective case.

"Well, darn. This OtterBox case was totally worth buying." I couldn't help but express my appreciation aloud.

After I looked up at the mountain, I hesitated and sat down on a nearby rock to reassess the situation. My eyes kept glancing at the phone in my hand. I wouldn't have an OtterBox case to protect me if I fell down. I had to make a choice and decided to recheck my climbing equipment.

Ice axe, no. Crampons, check. Harness, poor. Carabineers, check. Rope and cords, check. This about summed it up for me. I didn't have enough equipment to climb much farther. How anticlimactic.

I didn't know what I expected coming here, not knowing I'd need more. Maybe I expected a walk in the park or for the equipment to mysteriously appear out of thin air.

Looking back, I realized now I didn't think at all. I simply decided I'd go as far as I could. Nepal and Mount Everest were an accident. If it hadn't been for the last-minute change in Chinese visa laws, I wouldn't be here.

Was this going to be the end of my Mount Everest assent? Without a doubt, yes. I had to end this foolishness and stop. It would be different if I had the equipment to climb higher, but I didn't. I made the decision to turn back. At the very least, I could brag that my phone fell down Mount Everest and survived.

I faced the Mountain and whispered a few words of gratitude. I made a promise to my friends and family members to bring back small pieces of Mount Everest. I picked up several small granite and marble stones and placed them in my backpack. They would make the best gifts ever.

~*~*~

The first fifteen minutes of my return felt lonely and disheartening. Afterward, I picked up the pace. A headache reminded me that I needed to descend farther for it to get better.

I pushed myself harder and made good distance. I made it past Gorakshep and across the previous glacier. The glaring sun scorched my skin relentlessly, yet as hot as it was, the sheer cold air made me shiver. The cold clung to me like a broken heart. Nothing worked to distract it.

After the glacier, I lost my way and stumbled upon a glass pyramid building. It looked to be four to five-stories high. As I looked closer, solar panels covered the roof and walls. I concluded this was a research facility. It seemed crude, dark and abandoned, yet demanded my attention. At night, the building would make a perfect ghost hunting attraction.

I passed Lobuche and reached the next settlement called Dughla. Here I had to make a choice, to go back to Namche Bazaar using the same route as I climbed or take a different one. Looking at the map, I realized the new route took me to Namche quicker and offered different scenery. It didn't take long for me to decide. I took the new route.

The next settlement, Periche, welcomed me with colorful signs. The biggest one read, "Everest Marathon 2012! Welcome runners." Was this a running marathon? It didn't matter to me because I already felt like I had run one.

After I settled in the guesthouse and connected to Wi-Fi, I prepared myself for what was to come.

"Hi, Mom."

"Oh, thank God you called! I was worried sick. Where are you? Are you OK?"

"I'm still in Nepal. I'm doing well."

"Have you traveled enough? When are you coming back home?"

"Mom, I just started. I'll leave Nepal soon and go to China next. I'm not sure how long I'll be there."

"I'm glad you're well. Do you need money? Are the fish flying?"

"Mom! I'm OK. You don't need to ask me the secret question —if I've been abducted. I'm fine."

"Answer the question. Are the fish flying?"

"No. The fish are salted. There. Happy?"

"Oh, thank God. I'm so worried about you. You sure you have not been abducted or your money stolen?"

"No, Mom. I've not been abducted. Everything is good."

"Remember what I told you. Always keep your passport with you. Keep it next to your body. Stitch some cash into your underwear."

"Yes, Mom. I'll start stitching a pocket in my undies right away. Two hundred dollars should be enough. I'm sure the robbers won't think of checking there."

"Don't be funny, Aleksey. Now that you're done with your mountains, you need to call me every day. Do you understand?"

"You know I don't have telephone service here. I can only use Wi-Fi on my phone. However, I'll try to call more often. I'll also try to send you a text on Skype."

The brief conversations with my mother always followed the same pattern. I'm alive. I have money. I need to call again soon.

Outside the lodge, I saw several runners, with numbers strapped on their backs, jog into the settlement. They were all white foreigners. Several locals stood on the side to cheer them on. The runners didn't flood in by great numbers but trickled in one or two at a time.

I wanted to know more about this marathon.

"What is this Everest Marathon?" I asked the lodge owner, a middle-aged Nepalese man.

"Everest Marathon happens every year. Runners from all over the world join. The Extreme Ultramarathon is several days long and spans over sixty kilometers."

"Wow, sixty kilometers? Where do they start and finish?"

"It starts at Everest Base Camp and ends in Namche Bazaar. You've probably seen the red strings tied to trees, that's the path runners follow. It's longer and more difficult than the usual route climbers take."

I sighed. "The red strings. They bring back painful memories. I'll consider coming back in the future to run this marathon."

Chapter 23

The ringing of the alarm clock jolted me awake. I slammed my hand on the phone to silence the loud noise. My eyes struggled to stay open, but my mission was to reach Namche Bazaar today.

I dragged myself out of bed and into the bathroom to wash my face. The cold water never failed to refresh me. I stared at the brown wall in front of me. Would I ever see a mirror? I wanted to know how I looked. What monstrosity had I become after this exhausting adventure?

The large breakfast of beans and rice quickly digested in my stomach and supplied me with necessary energy. I stepped out of the lodge and onto the trail. Namche awaited.

Several Nepalese men with heavy backpacks joined me. Some jogged past, while others matched my pace.

I waved my hand at one of the young men. "Hi. Why is everyone rushing?"

He nodded and looked at my oversized green backpack with approval. "We carry bags for runners. Runners take long path, we take short path. We race, too."

Within fifteen minutes, six more bag carriers joined us. The faster ones broke away further, others lagged behind. My competitive personality wouldn't let them pass without a fight. I picked up the pace and rushed ahead to keep up with the pack of eight in front. To my advantage, they paid little attention to me.

After half an hour, fast walking turned into slow running. I tightened the straps on my backpack and raced onward. I occasionally noticed a glance and heard a laugh from other bag carriers, after which they usually picked up the pace to keep me trailing behind.

They could laugh all they wanted, but I would not lose them. After half an hour, I saw a village in the distance and passed it within ten breaths. None of the bag runners stopped either. I didn't bother to take out my map to check its name.

I picked up the pace again and left several of the bag runners in the dust. Catching up to the lead group, three of us ran side by side.

"Good job. Don't give up." The bag runner to my right gave a thumbs up and a smile.

I nodded with approval. If I tried to voice anything, I might bite my tongue off with the heavy backpack beating down on me with every step.

We passed another village, and I noticed some of the bag runners had slowed down. I took this opportunity to catch up and pass the ones in the lead. Some were unwilling and tried to persevere with a faster pace, but they could not persist for long. I pushed past them with a big grin on my face.

The strong muscles gained from my uphill climb trained me well. My body radiated endless vitality and an unwillingness to give up. The downhill slope also helped. I felt like a bull, challenging all who stood in my way.

I equipped my camelback at the lodge in the morning and didn't need to stop and drink water. I sipped from the tube while munching on snacks.

The villages flashed passed me, one after another. I moved with such zeal that I passed all of the bag runners and everyone else along the way. The direction to Namche looked simple, until I came to another fork in the road and followed the red strings.

This new route proved to be narrow, with a barely visible trail. I could no longer run and had to slow to a walk. Boulders stood in my way, and I had to navigate around them. Half an hour had gone by, and the bag runners had not caught up to me. I felt proud and laughed aloud. This only convinced me to pick up the pace.

Fifteen minutes later, I saw a Nepalese man walking toward me from the other direction. Something felt odd. I approached him and pointed ahead. "How far to the next village?"

He looked at my backpack and then back at me. "No, no. This take you to mountain. Ten kilometers more to village. Go back." He pointed to the steep route I took to get here. "Marathon runners run here."

I must have cringed so hard that the next moment he tapped my shoulders several times. "Don't give up. Go up."

No wonder there were no bag runners behind me. I had taken the wrong path after the last village. The damn red strings again. I turned around and grumbled as I slowly started the long uphill battle.

~*~*~

An hour had passed until the original trail came into view. The map confirmed my location. The disappointment ate at me. The bag runner's challenge would go down as a failure. My stomach protested and reminded me to stop and eat.

I looked around and saw a small, wood building with a "Ristorante" logo next to it. The patio outside had several tables, chairs and menus. Two men sat outside and one of them waved at me to join them.

The older of the two invited me to sit next to him.

"You were born in Russia? Look at that young man." The Nepalese man pointed to a blond-haired youth two tables away. "He's part of a Russian climbing group. The rest of the group is climbing farther. I'm bringing this young man back. He has altitude sickness."

"*Privet.*" I greeted the young man in Russian. He didn't look at me and continued to stare ahead.

The Nepalese man chuckled. "He won't understand you. He can't understand anyone at the moment. He's got the bad case of the sickness."

"You mean High-altitude Cerebral Edema?"

"If that's when brain swells with fluid, then yes. Russians are the most difficult climbers to deal with. They always carry vodka and drink too much. Alcohol is not good in high altitudes. Its effect is multiplied and bad for altitude adaptation," the Nepalese man explained.

I laughed. "That sounds about right with Russians. What else did you expect?"

"Drink is acceptable, but Russians often drink too much on the mountain. Someone gets sick and Russians leave him behind to get better on own. Not good because sick man cannot climb down alone. Need to be rescued later."

I understood the point he made. "I guess going alone is not a good idea, eh?"

"No. Get Sherpa or go with group, safer. Good way to check if you are getting bad altitude sickness is to do math. Do easy addition and multiplication. Try to remember your address and names of relatives. If you cannot do simple math problem, climb down fast. It won't be long until more serious problem come, and you'll be like him." He pointed to the Russian youth.

"Wow. That's useful information. Thank you." I got up and approached the young Russian. Although I stood in front of him, his eyes were wide open and clueless, like a newborn child. He seemed to have no awareness whatsoever.

A chill ran down my back. I could have fallen asleep and ended up like him and slowly died in my tent without even putting up a fight. What an awful way to go.

I finished my lunch, thanked the Nepalese man for his advice and continued to descend as I solved basic math problems.

~*~*~

Not long after, I stood at the entrance of a suspended walking bridge. A crowd had gathered waiting for a group of mules and yaks carrying equipment to cross. The animals walked in a line, one after another, wearing heavy packs.

I pushed through the crowd, not wanting to wait for the animals. My competitive personality motivated me to make it to Namche as soon as possible. Halfway across the bridge, I faced the lead yak. It kept moving as if I didn't exist. The yaks were much bigger up close and smelled like cow manure. Every step they took, the bridge shook. I held onto the rope on the side and moved out of their way.

The animals carried large sacks, and every time one passed,

it bumped into me. I felt like a twig in a storm. I had no control as the yaks kept moving without any concern for me. An exceptionally large yak bumped my body against the ropes and forced one of my feet to plunge off the side of the bridge. I barely held on to the metal cable with both hands as the animal made its way past me.

I persevered and slowly walked across. After I made it to the other side, everyone looked at me with a weird expression. Like, what was this fool thinking? I felt embarrassed but saved myself twenty minutes. At the moment though, I felt more like a mule than the mules.

After the bridge, the trail hugged the side of a mountain. Green colors of life started to become apparent. Trees and grasses of different kinds appeared nearby, and valleys below were full of lush forests.

Climbing down the mountain aggravated the blisters on my toes, but the descent eventually leveled and a valley greeted me. What I saw surprised me. Along a flowing river stood a perfect row of European style lodges. A clear-cut field of grass encircled them. The wooden, gable-roofed buildings offered balconies and a classy look. It clearly advertised accommodations to people who were willing to spend more.

It was good to have options, but somehow it felt intrusive. The beautiful valley no longer projected the feeling of Nepal but of Europe. These lodges must have been made for the group tours I'd seen from a distance. Foreigners of all ages, groups of medium to small sizes, trekked to different heights.

I soon envisioned the Mount Everest Base Camp trek populated by various star-ranked accommodations where people could have a home away from home, with all the comforts available. I shuddered at the thought and felt lucky to be here at this period of time before the culture was completely overshadowed by a more modern way of life.

~*~*~

As the day progressed, I saw a middle-aged Asian man taking pictures of the mountains, walking in the same direction.

I stopped next to him and looked at the scenery. "Beautiful." I tested his English.

"Yes. Very beautiful. I take many photos to show my family back in China."

I looked at him. "You're from China? Nice. I'm going to China soon. Want to walk together? It'd be great if I could ask you questions. I've never been there before."

He looked into the camera's viewfinder, adjusted the lens and took a shot of the broken branch lying on the ground. After the photograph, he faced me and smiled as we started our walk together. "No problem. I stop often to take pictures. I hope you won't mind. China is very big. What do you want to know?"

"Hmm. I love eating different foods. What kind of food should I try there? Is it as spicy as here? I also heard that food in China uses many chemicals. Is that true?"

"You asked the right person . . ." All of a sudden, he paused and framed another photo.

A few minutes later, he continued, "We have almost a billion and a half people in China. Our country has no choice but to chemically enhance foods, use growth hormones and recycle oils to feed all the people. Take vegetables for example. We soak them in bleach water for better appearance and to kill bacteria. We use many growth hormones to have the pigs grow faster and become fatter. What do you think happens when people eat them?"

I pondered. "But Chinese people are so skinny."

"In the countryside this is true, but in the cities, many are starting to get fat. The enhanced pigs are only a small example. Most Chinese use recycled oil, also called gutter oil. Many men and women go through dumpsters, trash bins, gutters and even sewers, scooping out liquid or solid refuse that contains used oil or animal parts. Then they process that into cooking oil, which they sell for a cheap price. It tastes very good."

I slowed down for a moment to understand. "You mean they pick up trash and make oil from it? Are you serious? Shouldn't that be illegal?"

My question hung in the air for ten seconds as I watched him concentrate on another photograph.

"Not only illegal, but bad for health. The government doesn't care. Everyone uses it. But when hungry, anything will do. Be careful of street food."

I grumbled. "But I like street food. It's one of the highlights of my travels. Eating is fun."

"Street food in China is the best, but you'll probably get sick if you eat it right away. A stomach needs up to a month to adjust to new bacteria. At the very least, try not to eat street food for the first two weeks, you should be fine then."

He was a wealth of information, and I wanted to ask him more to help dispel some myths about Chinese food. "I heard that Chinese street markets sell insects to eat. Do they sell scorpions? Ever since I saw Les Stroud on his *Survivorman* show eat a scorpion kabob, I wanted to eat one too. As I heard the crunchy sounds when he chewed the scorpion, my mouth salivated for some reason."

I turned and realized that I had been talking to myself. My new friend stopped walking a while back and stood taking pictures of yet another mountain peak.

After a few minutes, he caught up. "Did you say insects? Yes, Beijing street market is most famous for this, but many cities sell insects too. All insects taste the same when fried. Remember recycled oil? Do you . . ." he stopped in mid-sentence and prepared to take a picture of yet another mountaintop. There were so many.

"You weren't kidding when you said you'll be taking lots of pictures," I muttered under my breath.

If you can't beat them, might as well join them. I took out my camera, stood next to him and photographed away.

When we continued walking, I asked more questions. "I heard people eat animal brains in China. Do you know anything about it?"

"Oh, yes." He wiped the drool from his lower lip. "Pig brains are the best. With enough salt and spices, it's so delicious. In

China, we eat every part of the animal—brains, tongues, eyes, ears, hooves and everything possible. Nothing is wasted."

He paused for a moment and looked me in the eyes. "When you are in China, eat anything you want. Locals who eat this food their whole lives suffer health problems, but you'll be there for a short time. A month or two of eating this food won't create problems. Enjoy it. Otherwise you'll worry too much. You only live once."

His wisdom made me feel better. "You're right. Is there any food you recommend in China?"

He rubbed his chin in thought and smiled wickedly. "There is a local delicacy in south China you should try. It's not only a delicacy but is considered to have many medicinal benefits." He paused for a moment and stared at me.

"That's interesting. What is it?" I wanted to know.

"It's eggs boiled in the urine of young virgin boys. It's very popular in the south." He waited for my reaction.

I stayed silent for several seconds trying to process the information. "What? Seriously? Are you for real?"

His wide grin approved my response. "Oh yes, very serious. Although, it's not as popular as I made it out to be. It can still be found in some street markets."

I failed to find a proper response to this and changed the topic. "How are the police? Are they safe?"

"Police . . . are good to foreigners. You won't have a problem. It's different for locals."

We talked together for over an hour, stopping countless times so he could take more pictures of the same mountaintop from all possible angles. I didn't find anything special about it. It looked like hundreds of others. I guessed beauty was in the eye of the beholder.

~*~*~

I wanted to make it to Namche before sunset. I thanked him for all the useful information and moved on ahead.

By evening, I reached Namche Bazaar without much difficulty. I didn't venture to the village center but stayed in the outer parts.

After I paid for the room, I connected to the free Wi-Fi on my phone. That very moment many messages popped up, "Happy Birthday Aleksey!!!"

I had completely forgotten today's date, November twenty-two, my birthday. How fortunate for me to finish my journey on this day. I'd made it to Mount Everest and back. I couldn't think of a better gift for myself.

Last winter I spent my birthday in a lonely, cold room in Ireland. I couldn't ask for anything more at the time. Two years before, I was in the wilderness of Canada. This year, in Nepal climbing Mount Everest. I wondered where I'd spend my next birthday.

The next hour I talked to my family and replied to messages. I felt too tired to indulge myself in a birthday feast and ordered the cheap rice and beans. Since I finished my Mount Everest climb early, I still had four days before my scheduled flight to Kathmandu. It seemed like I didn't need to change the flight after all.

Chapter 24

After breakfast, I departed for Lukla. I remembered it to be a small mountain village with an airport. I'd fly from there to Kathmandu.

Once I started the trail, I charged like a bull. A belly full of food gave me the strength I needed. Halfway to Lukla, people congested the trail to the point where I had to stand in line to get through the bridges. This didn't stop me from pushing my way through and passing everyone.

I ran past the hikers and locals alike. No one got ahead of me. Sweat ran down my back. It didn't feel like the sweat produced from effort but more like a refreshing spring cooling me down.

After several kilometers of the uphill climb, I saw a familiar figure, the Chinese man I met the day before.

I tapped him on his shoulder. "It's good to see you again. You must have started early."

"Ah, hi. It's good to see you, too."

"What is your name? I didn't ask you yesterday. My name is Aleksey."

"It's Sha'a."

The moment he finished the sentence, I stopped to photograph a mountain.

"It's nice to meet you Sha'a. What's your job back in China?"

"I'm an architect. You?"

"Tour guide. Let's head to Lukla together?"

"OK."

Today it was my turn to stop and take photographs every few minutes. After an hour, we only progressed one kilometer. The scenery of the snow-capped mountains fascinated me, and I wanted to capture their beauty.

Sha'a and I had a silent photography session. In my head, in order to win, I had to put on the heat and photograph every other tree and interesting blades of grass.

Sha'a followed me and grumbled. "Is this what I do? Now I understand how it feels to stop every minute to take a photo."

I looked away and grinned. I wanted to laugh, but it would be rude. I proudly sang a silent victory.

Upon our entrance into Lukla, we saw a small Buddhist temple. It had a ten-foot prayer wheel inside. Sha'a's eyes lit up like fireflies on a moonless night. With a seamless, practiced motion, he reached for his camera and disappeared into the building.

I knew I wouldn't see him anytime soon. "Sha'a, I'm going to go find a place for the night. I'll see you later," I called out.

He stuck his head out the door. "I enjoyed walking with you. I'll stay here for a while. May we meet again."

~*~*~

I saw several buildings on the side of the road followed by a cluster of houses. Different signs advertised guesthouses in the area. The closer I came to the center of Lukla, the more crowded it became. Foreigners with backpacks swarmed the streets.

To my right I saw a three-story lodge. It had a small, grassy courtyard with tables and chairs. All of them were filled with foreigners who appeared to be drinking coffee.

I planned to spend the next four days in Lukla. My desire to save money on accommodations persuaded me to shop around for the best price.

After fifteen minutes of visiting different lodges, I finally saw the small airport sign and an enormous line outside one of the doors. I guessed this to be the airport registration office.

I approached an older couple at the end of the line. "Hi. What's the big line for?"

The man looked at me. "We're waiting to see if tomorrow's flights have been cancelled. The weather is bad. Most of the flights for the past week have been delayed. With luck, two or three planes will leave before ten in the morning but none after."

I worried. "Cancelled? Bad weather? Darn, I have a flight in four days. I hope it gets better by then."

"I doubt it. I've been delayed by two days already. It's unlikely that we'll leave tomorrow. I recommend you get in line and see if you can push your flight earlier."

"Thanks for the advice. I'll get in line then. Where did you both trek to?" I glanced at the quiet woman next to him.

He smiled. "No problem. We trekked to the Everest Base Camp but couldn't reach it. I'm worried about the flight out of here. Did you know that Lukla is one of the top ten most dangerous airports in the world? In fact, according to many sources, it's ranked as the third most dangerous."

"You serious? What makes it so dangerous? I flew in plenty of aircrafts. Large, small and even survived an airplane crash landing back in the US. How much worse can this be?" I asked.

"You survived an airplane crash? Wow. Lucky you. Despite the mumbo-jumbo that the airline companies came up with, a ninety-five percent airplane crash survival rate, the actual rate of survival in a real plane crash is less than twenty percent. You did good. This airport is dangerous because every year there are several crashes. Needless to say, many lives were lost."

I thought about his answer. "Yet, here we are. Fighting our way in line. Ironic, isn't it?"

He laughed. "Yeah, it is. At least we are not in Gibraltar airport. It's south of Spain, and due to the lack of space, the airplane has to cross a busy highway. Can you imagine having to cross a highway with fast moving cars as the airplane lands? It's also one of the top ten most dangerous airports."

"You know your airports. I'll give you that. This reminds me of the weird, solar-paneled pyramid I'd seen while descending Everest Base Camp. Do you know anything about it?"

"Do you mean *The Pyramid International Laboratory-Observatory*? I've only heard about it. It's there to study the environment, climate and other things. It's also a laboratory where researchers go. That building is a popular attraction. I've heard that some visitors make it their destination and then return."

For the next half an hour, we shared stories until their turn came.

"It was nice talking to you. I'm glad you joined us in line. The time passed by faster. Good luck on your travels." After farewells, he and his partner walked to the counter.

A Nepalese man on the other side of the counter looked at me. "Next."

"Hi. I have a flight to Kathmandu on November twenty-six. I've been told many flights have been cancelled. I'd like to see if I can get an earlier flight."

The man's hair was tousled, his eyes red and he looked tired. "Your reservation papers."

I handed him a printed copy of my flight manifest.

He glanced at it. "You're on the third plane leaving for Kathmandu, on the twenty-sixth, at eight thirty in the morning. If you change now, you'll be placed on a tenth plane leaving tomorrow and probably won't fly out anytime soon. I suggest you keep your confirmed flight."

I worried about my connecting flight to China. "I'll take your recommendation and keep my flight. Thank you."

He nodded and called out to the person behind me. "Next."

The evening encroached upon me, and I no longer cared where I stayed. I picked the closest, most rundown lodge near the airport. A three-story, moldy looking building fit the criteria of cheap—even by Nepal standards. The price didn't disappoint.

The room barely fit a chair, and the small bed didn't have a blanket. At the very least, it had a porthole-sized window. Despite the lack of a power outlet, a chair in the corner seemed like a bonus luxury item.

After unpacking and settling in, I went to the kitchen and ordered pasta with tomato sauce. I watched the young woman prepare the sauce using fresh tomatoes. It tasted heavenly.

After dinner, I walked through the town and glanced around for snacks and Sha'a. I smiled as I imagined him still taking pictures of the temple.

At the end of the day, I wrote in my journal and noted the day's highlights.

Chapter 25

A loud banging noise jolted me awake. My eyes opened quickly and my heart raced. Where was I? The loud banging started again. It must be coming from the kitchen, I thought. It sounded like a wooden stick hitting a hard, wet carpet.

It reminded me of my grandma's meat tenderizing process. As a child, I watched her hammer a piece of meat on a wooden board to soften it up. She then spiced and floured it before cooking.

What a wonderful, restful morning. Other than the kitchen preparing breakfast in the next room, I felt at peace.

Bang. Bang. Bang.

The loud noise sounded like machine gunfire. It hurt my ears. I needed to find a different room.

I dressed, left the lodge and searched for a new accommodation. The lodges on the main street were too expensive. I changed my search strategy and walked down an alley. Immediately, a lodge sign greeted me, "Homely Inn." Jackpot.

The owner of this small lodge offered a reasonable price. After I confirmed the existence of an outlet and complimentary Wi-Fi, I paid for the room, brought my equipment in and wrote down a mission statement for the day, "Eat tasty food."

Having finished the climb four days sooner, I had extra spending money. Converting cash to Chinese yuan for the next leg of my journey wouldn't be financially viable. Besides, going on a snack-eating spree sounded incredibly appealing.

I let go of my spending limitation mindset and purchased all the good-looking snacks I saw in the outdoor markets. I went into various hole-in-the-wall restaurants and tasted different meats and salted vegetables, which seemed to be extremely popular in Nepal, and drank at least eight cups of *chai*, tea with milk.

By the afternoon, my stomach felt bloated. The very

thought of sweets and snacks made me feel nauseated. I hoped I wouldn't get sick again, but it felt so good to have a full stomach. Gluttony, my nemesis, had gotten the better of me once again.

Back at the lodge, I called my parents. I also received good news about my Cambodian friend's arranged marriage. It seemed his new wife wanted children. It made me wonder who'd be the boss in their family. I congratulated him and wished them many kids.

My smelly clothing started to turn heads on the streets and convinced me to wash up. I also had to get ready for the next step of my journey, China.

Upon request, the older Nepalese owner gave me a bucket. I went out back, behind the lodge, and used a hose to fill it with ice-cold water, the only option available. I then took all my dirty clothing and dumped them in.

After half an hour of hand washing, the owner walked out. "You are very good to wash your equipment. I see many climbers come back and continue to wear dirty shirts and socks. They are lazy and don't do anything. The house always smells. You did good."

For some reason I felt proud. "Thank you."

~*~*~

With a few hours of remaining daylight, I decided to explore the village farther. After walking through several streets, I heard the familiar sound of a paddle hitting a small plastic ball.

I turned at the corner and saw two Nepalese boys playing Ping-Pong. The kids demonstrated skill beyond their age. After their game, the loser of their round smiled at me, then handed me the paddle. "You. Play," he said.

"Thank you." I accepted it and waited for the young man to start the game. His eyes tensed as he drew the paddle back, and then hit the ball full swing. With great speed, the ball bounced toward me.

The familiar anticipation of the first hit of the game exhilarated me. Despite the ball's speed, I knew where I had to hit it.

I tightened the paddle in my hand and hit the ball perfectly. It bounced back to his side and our game started.

Despite my loss, the game proved to be a good warm up. I gave my paddle back and waited for the next round.

Half an hour had passed. A blond, middle-aged man approached the table. "Can I join?"

"Sure. You can play the next game. I'll skip my turn." I pushed the paddle toward him.

"No, no. That's OK. I'll wait for—"

"Play. We be back." The older of the two boys handed the foreigner his paddle.

I watched the boys run into a nearby house. "OK. I guess we can play now," I said.

After two intense games, we were at a draw. The third round was about to start, but I couldn't help but share a story. "You're good. I've not played for more than a year but love the game. I worked on a cruise ship a few years back, and we had a Ping-Pong table in the gym. Playing Ping-Pong on a ship is the best." I served.

He returned the ball with a spin on it. "Is it because you played the game with all the hot girls?"

I smiled. "That's funny, but the table was located in a crew gym. Can you imagine playing Ping-Pong in a storm? Just as the ball is about to make a corner shot, a big wave tilts the table and the ball misses. It adds a certain edge to the game—a touch of the unknown. It improved my game play big time."

He hit the ball back to me but it got caught in the net. "Damn it. Another game?" he asked.

"Sure."

After an hour, the two Nepalese boys returned, and we handed the paddles back. I thanked them for their trust, and then walked back to the lodge. Along the way, I passed the airport office. The line of people had doubled in size. It seemed like getting a flight out of Lukla had become a lottery.

~*~*~

At the lodge, I met a group of three young people in the kitchen. With pleasantries out of the way, we ordered dinner and shared a few words about ourselves. They were from Israel and awaited their flight to Kathmandu.

The youngest Israeli man called out to the host in the kitchen, who approached with a look of anticipation. "Yes? Would you like a beer?"

"No, no. We are from Israel. We don't drink alcohol. Three waters please."

The host's mouth closed and the light in his eyes dimmed, like a candled blown away by a breeze from an open window. He looked like a depressed bar owner who only served soft drinks. How was he going to make any money? He came back with three waters.

I couldn't resist and asked one of the men, "Do people in Israel not drink alcohol?"

"We are Muslim, and over eighty percent of Arabs in Israel are Muslim. We are prohibited from drinking alcohol."

His words surprised me. "Wow. I didn't know that. Great job staying strong and not drinking."

"Thank you, but in recent years many teenagers have broken this rule and get drunk, especially young women. Many of my friends got into trouble."

"Thank you for sharing."

The young man nodded and continued sipping his water. After a few minutes, the three of them closed their eyes and started to sing a song in their native tongue. They occasionally looked up and raised their hands with palms facing up.

Their song entertained me for several minutes until the aromatic smell of beans and rice wafted from the kitchen. My stomach grumbled, as if demanding it.

The host came out and let us know the food would be served soon. I raised my hand to get his attention and brought an imaginary cup to my lips.

, He approached, then asked, "You want water as well, yes?" I saw the sour look in his eyes, like an unprepared man who bit into a tart, juicy lemon.

I understood his pain and smiled. "No, I want a local beer."

The man's mouth hung open for more than a second before showing me the brightest smile I'd seen the whole day. "Coming right up."

Although the beer cost three hundred rupees, about three and a half dollars, the owner's happy expression made it worthwhile.

A moment later, he returned and held the lonely tin can with both hands. With an exaggerated wave, he placed the San Miguel beer in front of me. "Enjoy." His voice was loud enough to be heard at the other tables.

I looked at the Israelis to my right, but they continued singing without a care. The host returned with a smile and placed the first plate of beans and rice in front of me. Only then, were the other plates served to the Israelis. Who would have thought that a simple beer would have made such a loyal friend?

The beans and rice were excessively spicy. This changed the flavor of the San Miguel to an India *Pale Ale*, with its bitter taste. The IPA's bitterness originated from using more hops and preservatives, made for British troops stationed in India in the nineteenth century. The accidental side effect soon became a sensation.

Despite the distasteful beer, for some reason it felt good to drink. Did that even make any sense? I didn't drink often, but at times, it was one of the most enjoyable pleasures.

After dinner, I stayed in the kitchen and kept to myself. With ear buds in place and a second beer in hand, I wrote in my journal.

At the moment, I wanted to get a buzz and write dramatic things. My last year's journey through Ireland revealed that some of the greatest writers in history were probably inspired by loneliness, misery and alcohol. Mixing all three together, made the perfect cocktail for an emotional, depressing, yet inspirational, work.

Besides, could truly passionate stories have been written without any emotion? It would probably be more like drinking decaf coffee—the taste was there but something was missing.

The journal stole all of my attention. Like a lover, I held it in one hand and tenderly stroked words onto the paper with the other. Ever so carefully, yet passionately, my thoughts, feelings and dreams appeared before my eyes, like oils on canvas.

By the time I finished writing, the night had grown dark. I looked around, only to find the kitchen empty. It was time for bed.

Chapter 26

I awoke to the sound of soft voices coming from outside my door. It felt nice to laze about without a reason to get up. My eyes slowly opened, but the bright light blinded me. I shut them until they adjusted to the waking world.

After breakfast, my day began with a ten-minute walk to the airport. A six-foot fence surrounded it. Inside, a short runway stretched for five hundred meters, around seventeen hundred feet.

To my surprise, the runway continued to the very end until it reached a cliff and then dropped off. Beyond that, thick fog permeated the air making the view of the mountain ahead barely visible.

The tiny airport held four *Tara* airplanes. Each had eight rows of windows, making it similar in length to a school bus. Six people climbed a small ladder and boarded a plane. The expression exhibited by one of the women showed concern, to say the least.

I watched her pause at the door and hold onto the side of the entrance with both hands. A man behind patted her shoulder and urged her to continue. Several minutes later, airport staff loaded their luggage, along with several large boxes into the side compartments, filling them to the limit.

When everything looked ready, the airplane taxied to the start of the runway. The thundering propellers rotated faster every moment, forcing me to cover my ears. The pilot released the brakes, and the tires screeched as the plane jerked forward.

The short five hundred meters disappeared in a matter of seconds, but the plane's tires were still on the ground. My heart beat faster as I watched the airplane reach the end of the runway and dive down the edge of the cliff. Seconds later, it swooped up into the sky.

My relief was short-lived as I watched the plane make a

sharp left in order to avoid crashing into the mountain ahead. A moment later, the flying apparatus disappeared into the thick fog and maneuvered through the mountain valleys. Cold sweat ran down my back. I knew I had to fly out the same way the next morning and shuddered.

The pain in my fingers brought me back to reality. My knuckles were white from holding onto the fence too hard. I relaxed and noticed several other backpackers, who stood beside me. Some had worried looks, while others displayed their excitement.

For the remainder of the day, I explored the small village, then in the evening, I returned to the lodge. Before bed, I went to the kitchen, plugged in my phone and enjoyed the role-playing video game, "Inotia 4."

The story revolved around an assassin and his target, a priestess of the light. They had now fallen in love and were fleeing from the bad people. I strongly believed in happy endings and played the whole evening to help them successfully escape.

Chapter 27

My body shivered with cold as I stood in darkness outside the closed airport doors. My watch showed six in the morning, yet I didn't see a soul in sight. Was I in the right place? My heart beat faster with worry that I'd missed the flight.

The wet, wool sweater sucked the warmth out of my body because it hadn't dried. To stay warm, I jumped up and down. Getting sick was not an option.

After several minutes, I saw a young man with a backpack. He approached me. "Is this the right place for the airport departures?" he asked.

I shrugged. "I don't know but hope so."

Fifteen minutes later, the doors to the airport opened, and a Nepalese man invited us inside. By now, several people had lined up behind me. I checked in at the desk and submitted my backpack. The freshly printed ticket indicated my airplane to be the third for departure.

"Wait there," the man said, then pointed to a different room.

I entered and sat in one of the many available red, plastic chairs. The room had two glass doors leading to the runway, with signs indicating Gate One and Gate Two. A third sign, in the corner of the room, attracted my attention. The words "Tea Stall" were slobbered onto a cardboard box. Below it stood an empty plastic table.

As I dreamed of a hot beverage, a man walked in and placed a thermos, powdered coffee and tea packets on the table. Like well-trained soldiers, everyone in the room formed a straight line to get refreshments.

The warm paper cup thawed my fingers as more people arrived. To my surprise, almost all the faces were familiar. We'd crossed paths these past few days in Lukla or during the climb.

For the next half hour, I socialized with everyone in the room. The older couple from New Mexico, the two young

Frenchmen who'd taught me the 'Nepalese Guy' card game and others. They met my enthusiasm as we shared stories of our accomplishments and pains.

~*~*~

After the first two airplanes took off, an airport employee walked into the room. "Third plane is delayed until the weather gets better," he announced. Loud grumbles spread throughout the room.

Fifteen minutes later, the same man came back. "Third plane is ready. Please line up by Gate One and proceed to the airplane when the doors open. Do not walk under the propeller as you board."

We went outside and boarded the airplane. To my surprise, the seats were aligned in rows of three, with a total of eighteen. I drew the lucky straw and sat next to a window.

The airplane doors closed. I looked into the open cockpit and observed the pilot and co-pilot starting the plane. The propellers spun, slowly at first. Their rotation increased until the airplane shook, then roared to life, like a bear awakened.

I tried to comfort myself, remembering the countless flights I'd flown on similar, smaller airplanes. The memories didn't help. My stomach churned and the familiar feeling of worry arose.

The pilot released the brakes and we pushed forward with a jerk. I felt my body lean back against the seat. Through the window, I saw the runway ending and rechecked my seatbelt to prepare for a downward plunge.

Both hands gripped the seat handles as I eyed the approaching drop off. I heard the front wheels roll off the runway with a thump, followed by a sharp dip down. A moan escaped my lips as gravity pulled at me. Seconds later, I felt the nose of the airplane pull up as the thundering propellers overtook any yells I may have made.

Before I could celebrate the successful liftoff, the airplane made a sharp left, and my body rolled hard against the seat. Countless ups and downs made me feel like a shaken martini.

My empty stomach thanked me for not eating a large breakfast.

With every bump from the turbulent air, I felt the tea slosh around in my belly, until I dug frantically into the back of the seat in front of me for a souvenir bag. Behind me, I heard someone vomit.

After ten minutes of the airborne rollercoaster ride, we were above many of the mountains and flew smoothly through a large valley. I held tightly to the empty, plastic vomit bag, not willing to risk putting it back in place.

A young flight attendant in the first row unbuckled her seatbelt and pulled out a Ziploc bag from a drawer. She walked through the aisle and kindly offered everyone a mint candy. Her lower lip shook as she forced a smile. The fear in her eyes overshadowed any comfortable words she offered. She must have been new.

I chewed on the mint candy and remembered my friend's wisdom about it helping to relieve motion sickness. After fifteen minutes, I saw Kathmandu below and felt the airplane rattle in descent.

~*~*~

My stomach settled as soon as my foot hit the tarmac. I wanted to kiss the ground but decided to collect my luggage instead. Afterward, I walked out of the stuffy terminal and into the busy streets outside the airport. Dozens of Nepalese hands grabbed for me and my luggage, offering a taxi ride.

After I confidently declined overpriced offers, the crowd thinned. Taxi drivers received a commission for every foreigner they brought to a travel agency or hotel. They were probably looking for travelers who were starting, not ending, their Nepal journey.

I finally negotiated a cheap taxi ride to the North Thamel Elbrus Hostel. Its price and location, in the touristy area of the city, appealed to me.

The young driver didn't say much and only spoke upon our arrival. "Hostel there." He pointed to a busy, narrow street. "Difficult to drive. Please walk. OK? You see sign on left soon."

I didn't want him to suffer through the narrow road. "No problem. I'll walk. Thank you."

After paying, I pushed through the crowded street filled with small, dirty one-room stores selling everything from snacks to toiletries. The vibrant red, pink and blue decorative patterns outside the shops fascinated me as I admired the culture's bright atmosphere.

The spicy smells wafting from the restaurants tempted my now calm stomach to try the local delicacies. People came and went, like waves on a shore. They pushed, shoved, yelled and stared.

The change in pace reminded me of the pleasures of civilization. The long period of solitude starved me for good company, as well as a tasty meal.

I checked in at the hostel for one thousand rupees, about twelve dollars. A friendly clerk gave me a map of the city and highlighted my next stops.

After unpacking, I left the room and went to find Paul, the Nepalese man who'd helped me during the first day in the country.

I dodged cars and beeping motorbikes as I made my way through the narrow streets. The eager street hawkers greeted me at every corner, and loud mayhem confused my senses. The maze of nameless streets teemed with excitement and life.

After fifteen minutes, the map proved to be useless. Instead, I followed the compass on my watch, which guided me in the direction of a main street, and then I oriented myself from there.

Paul's office sign stood unchanged, yet I looked at it with different eyes than the first time, a month ago. My perception had changed, but it wasn't long before the streets around me felt more comfortable, as if I belonged to them. The foreign faces weren't as mysterious and even the piles of trash complemented the view.

I had finally integrated into the Nepalese culture. It was no longer beyond my comprehension. I had lived their culture and experienced their ways of life—although only a small part of it, but more than a casual traveler.

I was not a tourist sitting on a bus watching passively as people around me lived away their lives. I delved deeper and talked to them, lived with them and ate their food. I saw their way of life, not through rose-colored glasses, but experienced Nepalese hardships.

They no longer looked like strangers to me but people with whom I could relate. I imagined their stories and painted a picture in my mind of their daily activities.

A feeling of accomplishment warmed my heart. I had succeeded in traveling through Nepal and could now remove the country from my "To Travel" list. I'd been here. I'd done what I wanted. It was time to move on.

~*~*~

A loud honking noise awoke me from my daydream. I looked to my right and saw a Nepalese man flipping his middle finger and yelling at me to move away from the middle of the road.

"Sorry." I waved my hand and finished crossing the street. It seemed like I needed to pay better attention where I daydreamed, or I'd become a statistic rather than a visitor of Nepal —one of the many foreigners to be run over by a moving vehicle.

I took the stairs to the second floor and entered Paul's three-room office. Instinctively, I looked through the open door and saw him talking to a blond-haired young man. Paul noticed me, nodded his head and motioned for me to wait.

I sat at one of the available chairs in the waiting area and looked around. The familiar travel posters of Mount Everest no longer looked as majestic as when I first saw them. The Mountain no longer seemed like an uncharted territory meant for a select few. I had set my foot on it. And that made the poster exactly what it was, an oversized photograph of a mountain hanging on a wall.

Was this arrogance, wisdom, or experience? I decided to think about this at a later date. The act of self-discovery fascinated me. Approaching footsteps brought me back to the moment at hand.

"This is Aleksey. He used my services in the past. Aleksey, how was your Everest trip?" Paul asked as he led the young man out of his office.

"Hi, Paul. It's good to see you again. The climb was awesome. Thank you for helping me previously. Your arrangements worked out perfectly." I told the truth and wanted to support Paul by voicing my response to the man next to him.

"I'm glad you're back safely. I'll be with you soon." Paul guided the man to the exit. "Frank, please come back tomorrow and you'll meet your Sherpa. Take care."

Paul closed the door behind Frank and faced me. "I'm glad you came. Tell me of your experiences. Did you have a good time?"

I told Paul about my journey to Mount Everest until I reached the Base Camp, but not after. The attempt to climb further without a permit would get me in trouble.

Paul clapped his hands together. "Wow, well done. You made it all the way to the Base Camp on your own. You deserve a prize." He opened a drawer in his desk and pulled out a paper. "This is a certificate stating that you reached Everest Base Camp and climbed the height of five thousand five hundred and fifty meters. A small memento from me."

After handing me the certificate, Paul shared a business proposition. If I recommended anyone to his office, I'd get a small percentage of the total amount the client purchased. I accepted his offer, thanked him again and reached for the exit door. After all, I still had a lot to do.

~*~*~

On my way to the Yak Restaurant for lunch, I explored the local markets to buy gifts for my friends and family. This month's experience in Nepal taught me the importance of bargaining. Most street vendors did not speak English, but the language of money is universal.

"Kati?" I picked up a shawl at one of the stands and asked for the price.

The man replied in Nepali. I didn't understand, took out pen and paper, and then motioned for him to write the amount. He understood and jotted down a number. I looked at it, frowned and shook my head. I crossed out his offer and wrote down half its price.

He raised his hands and looked up, as if praying to Allah. I didn't need to speak the language to know he didn't agree with my counter offer. He took the paper back, crossed out my offer and wrote a higher amount. The negations continued until we settled on a price.

At another street vendor, I pointed to a beautiful, pink shawl. "Kati?"

"Hello, my friend," the vendor said in English. "The price is written below. Here, have a look." He pointed at the price tag.

I glanced at the amount. The last shawl I purchased was less expensive. I stood silent for a moment, contemplating the counter offer.

"It's OK, my friend. Only the best price for you. Let me lower it." He typed a number on the calculator.

I grimaced and stood silent comparing the price with the last purchase. I frowned and felt cheated because the previous vendor charged me more.

"Still not happy with the price? Don't worry so much. Here." He typed a smaller number again.

"Wow." I widened my eyes and looked back at him in surprise.

He hesitated for a moment. "OK. OK. I'll make it cheaper just for you, but no more. This is the lowest I can go." He took back the calculator and reduced the price again.

I paid him, "Thank you." I guessed that sometimes, silence was the best way to bargain.

A few streets from the Yak Restaurant, I saw a store selling various decorative swords and knives. I wanted to get my friend a post-wedding gift. A large knife or a sword seemed like a manly and sensible gift. Or did it? I pondered this for a moment and decided, at the very least, to explore the wares.

The moment I stepped into the store my eyes glittered with excitement. Swords and knives covered the walls and glass displays.

"Welcome. Please look around and let me know if you have any questions," a man called out from behind the counter.

After fifteen minutes of browsing, I chose two knives and brought them to the cashier.

He unsheathed the weapons. "These are excellent choices. The one to your right is a Kukri and the better choice of the two. It has an inverted curved blade, used in Nepal as both a weapon and a machete. It's a decorative knife. Take a look at the beautiful, handcrafted artwork on the blade." He pointed at the carvings on the Kukri. "It makes a perfect gift."

"You convinced me, but I do not have enough cash with me to buy it."

"It's OK, my friend. How much do you have?"

I took out all the rupees from my wallet and gave them to him.

He counted the bills and smiled. "You have a little more than half the price of the knife, but it's enough. Take the knife, and think of it as a gift from Nepal. Is this all the money you have left?"

"Thank you. Yeah, I'm leaving Nepal soon, and this is all I have left. I can withdraw more money later, though."

"No. Don't do that. I don't want to take everything you have. Here." He gave me back two of the larger bills. "Please come back to Nepal and tell your friends about our country. We want more people to visit us and be happy."

I grinned. "This will definitely not be my last visit to Nepal. It's a beautiful place with wonderful people. You did not have to do this, but thank you. This money will be enough. If I get the chance, I'll tell others about your shop." I picked up the knife and marveled at the excellent post-wedding gift.

~*~*~

A few blocks later, the Yak Restaurant seemed the same as I remembered it. I went inside, found a seat and looked through the menu. To celebrate my final day in Nepal, I chose *Tongba*, a millet-based, traditional local alcohol drink, with a yak sizzler as an entree.

In a few minutes, the server put a bamboo cup with a straw on my table and smiled. "Enjoy. Tongba is our specialty. Drink it all."

I looked into the steaming cup and no longer felt the thirst for the drink that I'd had a moment ago. Small brown grains with tiny black dots at the center of each immediately reminded me of eyeballs. Hundreds of them looked at me. I supposed they were pieces of millet.

"Here goes nothing." I mumbled and sucked on the straw. One sip was all it took for me to stop. The warm liquid stayed in my mouth while I debated whether to spit it back in the cup or run to the bathroom.

But then, I remembered my Russian friend's wise words. "Real men don't complain or make faces when drinking alcohol. Drink this glass of vodka and don't cringe again. It's unbecoming of you." His words echoed in my mind as my expression calmed and I swallowed the bitter drink. It took all my willpower not to shudder and grimace.

With a blank expression, I sprinkled salt on my hand and licked it as a bear would a honeycomb with relentless desire and anticipation.

I stared back at the nearly full cup of Tongba and prepared myself for the battle ahead. Like my drinking friend from the past had said, "Real men finish their drinks." The challenge was on.

As I stepped out of the restaurant, I tried to shake off the bitter taste. I wasn't sure what was more difficult, getting to Mount Everest or finishing a drink of Tongba. Yet both had something in common, I finished what I had set out to do.

I looked at my map and noted the *UNESCO World Heritage Site, Durbar Square*, my next destination.

~*~*~

As I approached the center of Durbar Square, the narrow

streets filled with shops parted to make way for the old but majestic architecture. I glanced at an information sign and marveled at the idea of exploring over fifty temples, palaces, courtyards and a royal elephant stable.

I climbed atop one of the many larger temples and looked around. Rickshaws and the white *Maruti Suzuki* taxis surrounded the square. A temple stood in the center as lines of visitors awaited their turn to climb the stairs to the top.

At the square, a peculiar sign stood out. It showed a drawing of a man with a jacket over his shoulder peeing on a temple. A bright X over the sign indicated this to be wrong. I didn't realize that the amazing architecture of Durbar Square served as a popular outhouse for the locals.

I circled the top of the temple and admired a smaller temple below. Its roof had holes, and wooden poles supported the walls, yet it stood majestic as the setting sun glowed behind it, highlighting every edge and curve.

By the closed gate, lay a young man. He wore tattered clothing. His disheveled hair looked like a rat's nest. He had no interesting qualities about him, except the ever-moving concealed right hand in his pants. I paused for a moment to understand the situation.

The young man watched as people below him passed by. Every time he saw a woman, the hand in his pants rose and fell rapidly. When the specimen of desire left his view, his hand stopped. Some of the women noticed him and walked rapidly away as he stared at their backsides with drunken indifference.

This continued for several more minutes until a group of foreign women slowly walked by, oblivious to their surroundings as they chatted away. The young man atop the temple straightened his back with vigor and stared at a curly, blondhaired woman with fervor.

He only had several seconds before they left his field of vision, and the moment they passed by, the man's body shuddered as his head fell back with closed eyes.

Several seconds later, he picked up a bottle with his other

hand and drank a large chug of the content. After the drink, his body collapsed and he passed out, with the right hand still in his pants.

I shook my head at the sight below and continued exploring the Durbar Square until eventually making my way back to the hostel.

~*~*~

At the hostel, I stepped into the shower room, locked the door and hung my clothes. I turned the shiny, metallic dial and felt the warm water pour over my body as my mind faded into dullness. The heat soaked into my skin and I closed my eyes. My legs threatened to buckle from the sheer pleasure. Hot water was a luxury I hadn't been able to afford for a month.

As my skin drank in the water like a thirsty elephant, I caught my reflection in the mirror. The sound of the shower faded into the background, and the warmth of the water lost its allure. I stood baffled and stared at the reflection of a stranger.

After what seemed like an eternity, I finally saw the reason for my change. The reflection showed a skinny man with nothing but bones and thin muscles held together by a layer of skin.

My biceps were tightly wrung around the bone, like a twisted towel about to tear. Skin hugged my ribs so closely that I started to count them. How many ribs do humans have? I counted twelve on each side.

Before this journey, my six-pack was clearly visible and my chest pushed through my shirt. Even my butt looked well rounded, in a healthy kind of way.

Before Nepal, my shoulders stood out like a plate of armor. They now resembled a thick layer of leather clinging to shoulder bones. Only my legs resembled a memory of the past, but with proportions significantly more defined and compact than before. What had happened to my body?

The shower no longer offered the comfort it did a moment ago. Why had I lost so much weight? I reserved this sentiment for dinner as I concentrated on scrubbing away a months' worth of dirt and watched the gray water disappear through the drain beneath my feet.

~*~*~

After the shower, I walked to a local *momo* restaurant a few streets away. Momo are dumplings with various spiced fillings. They reminded me of Russian *pelmeni*, minus the spices. Russian food offers a very limited spice selection. Meat, vodka and potatoes are the staple.

The sun had set but the main roads were as bright as day. The streetlights illuminated the way. I walked into the momo restaurant and saw a mix of locals and young foreigners wearing dingy clothing.

Like many other restaurants, the costs of meals were not displayed. To gauge the prices, I decided to observe the locals for a few minutes before finding a seat.

The moment I took my first step, a man called out to me, "Hello, my friend. I am happy you come to my restaurant. We make delicious momo. Here, sit." He pulled out a chair at an empty table.

"Thank you. Your restaurant looks amazing. Momo are delicious. How much for a plate of chicken momo?"

"For you, my friend, I give local price, not tourist price. One hundred twenty-five rupees. You also get a soda. Sprite OK?"

"Wow, amazing price. Thank you." A plate of momo with a drink for under two dollars helped me stay within my limited cash budget.

"No problem. Where are you from and where do you go next in Nepal?"

"I'm from America and just finished the Everest trek. I'll go home tomorrow. Your momo restaurant will make a wonderful last dinner for me."

"Welcome back from trek. You make good memories? What do you think of Nepal?"

"Nepal is beautiful. The people are friendly and seem happy. The food is delicious. My favorite dish is dal bhat. I think I tried every version of it, and although I ate it every day, I miss it already."

The owner laughed. "If you wish, I can make you dal bhat now."

I shuddered at the thought. "That's kind of you, but I'll need a few days away from it to fully appreciate it again. Nepal is a country I will not forget. I'll return."

~*~*~

After the conversation, my momo was served. I fully concentrated on gaining weight, but that only lasted until the first bite. The dumplings were so spicy, only the texture of the chicken remained. Forget the flavor. I barely kept tears from flowing. Only the sweet soda helped calm the heat.

Back at the hotel I arranged for a taxi at the front desk, and then went to my room. There, a long list of unread emails required my attention. As I fully concentrated on catching up with my other life, I heard the familiar ring on my phone.

"Aleksey, buddy, I'm glad you're alive. I read your email and had to video call you. Glad you're on Skype now. How much weight did you lose?"

I laughed. "What's up, Daniel. It's good to see you. And here I felt all alone in my room with no one to talk to. I have no idea how much weight I lost but enough to scare me."

"You better be careful, Aleksey. The reason you lost so much muscle mass is because you depleted your body's glucose and fat. Afterward, the body starts to eat muscle to break down into amino acids for energy. To make it short, the body eats itself." Daniel sternly looked at me on the phone screen.

"Well, damn it. That sounds serious. No wonder. Does this muscle loss have any permanent effects?"

"Nah, it takes a while before permanent side effects set in. You'll be fine, but don't let this happen for long periods of time or you'll suffer problems later. I think it's called *catabolism*. Look it up online."

"Big thanks, Daniel. You always know how to make me feel better. I can now confidently say that I've got no fat on me. These are some big bragging rights."

We talked for few more minutes, and then I went to sleep.

My last thought was to consider carrying dehydrated food and protein bars at all times.

Chapter 28

As I sat in the comfortable airplane seat, I enjoyed a delicious third round of salmon and rice. I loved Air China. Although the flight only lasted an hour and twenty minutes, everyone received a full meal, with free refills. I ate ravenously and tried to fatten up.

The first part of my journey, Nepal, had ended. China was next. I didn't have plans for it, but eating and sleeping for a few days sounded good. A rested body and an extra pound of fat behind the belt would unveil my next destination.

The low altitude of the plane revealed the scenery below. A bridge stretched for miles across the sands of a desert. Countless little rivers snaked underneath, which flowed to the horizon. I strained my eyes but could not find a single vehicle on the bridge. Was it used for military purposes or simply a lonely road leading nowhere?

I didn't know why, but I wanted to walk across it. I wanted to hold the sand in my hands and watch it slowly trickle between my fingers. The very thought ignited a fire in my heart—I wished to explore, to feel, to seek adventures and overcome the tribulations they offered.

A piece of salmon slipped off my fork, dropped onto the plate and splattered oil on my jacket, but I didn't care. I continued to stare out the window and imprinted the scenery in my memory.

China. I would be there soon and do what my heart desired. I would find this bridge and walk across it.

But before confronting this bridge, I had a connecting flight to Lhasa, Tibet. Tibet held a special meaning in my heart. I thought of it as one of the last frontiers of adventure—a place of mystery and intrigue, with endless mountains leading to sacred monasteries. In my eyes, they held secrets that city folks, like myself, couldn't fathom.

The airport of Lhasa would give me a brief glimpse of this fascinating land. A smile slowly appeared on my face. New adventures awaited.

END OF BOOK 1

Stay tuned for Book 2: Adventures in Tibet

Note from the Author:

I hope you have enjoyed reading my book as much as I enjoyed writing it. If so, please take the time to write a short review on Amazon.

Thank you,

Aleksey

Glossary

Disclaimer: The definitions in this glossary are from Wikipedia, unless otherwise noted. This glossary is not intended to be used as a medical and or camping or hiking guide, nor does it in any way intended to promote religions or religious beliefs, products, brands names, foods, organizations, corporations or other.

The sole purpose of this glossary is to serve as a brief definition to help define some of the words used within this book and for no other purpose. These definitions are in no way complete. The reader is advised to further research each definition.

Italicized words are further explained in the glossary.

Acetazolamide: Sold under the trade name Diamox, among others, is a medication used to treat glaucoma, epilepsy, altitude sickness, periodic paralysis, idiopathic intracranial hypertension, and heart failure.

Air China Limited: The flag carrier and one of the major airlines of the People's Republic of China, with its headquarters in Shunyi District, Beijing.

Altitude sickness: The mildest form being acute mountain sickness (AMS), is the negative health effect of high altitude, caused by rapid exposure to low amounts of oxygen at high elevation. Symptoms may include headaches, vomiting, tiredness, trouble sleeping, and dizziness.

B movie or B film: A low-budget commercial motion picture that is not an arthouse film. In its original usage, during the Golden Age of Hollywood, the term more precisely identified films intended for distribution as the less-publicized bottom half of a double feature (akin to B-sides for recorded music).

Baldur's Gate: Baldur's Gate is a series of role-playing video games set in the Forgotten Realms Dungeons & Dragons campaign setting. The game has spawned two series, known as the Bhaalspawn Saga and the Dark Alliance, both taking place mostly within the Western Heartlands, but the Bhaalspawn Saga extends to Amn and Tethyr.

Biseptol: Trimethoprim/sulfamethoxazole (TMP/SMX), also known as co-trimoxazole, among other names, is an antibiotic used to treat a variety of bacterial infections. It consists of one part trimethoprim to five parts sulfamethoxazole. It is used for urinary tract infections, methicillin-resistant Staphylococcus aureus (MRSA) skin infections, travelers' diarrhea, respiratory tract infections, and cholera, among others.

Bloomberg, Michael: Michael Rubens Bloomberg KBE is an American businessman, politician, author, and philanthropist. As of April 2019, his net worth was estimated at $62.1 billion, making him the 6th-richest person in the United States and the 9th richest person in the world.

Boy Scouts of America: The Boy Scouts of America (BSA) is the largest scouting organization and one of the largest youth organizations in the United States, with about 2.3 million youth participants and about one million adult volunteers. The BSA was founded in 1910, and since then, about 110 million Americans participated in BSA programs at some time in their lives. BSA is part of the international Scout Movement and became a founding member organization of the World Organization of the Scout Movement in 1922.

Buddhist Monk: A bhikkhu (Pali; Sanskrit: bhikṣu) is an ordained male monastic ("monk") in Buddhism. Male and female monastics ("nun", bhikkhuni, Sanskrit bhikṣuṇī) are members of the Buddhist community. The lives of all Buddhist monastics are governed by a set of rules called the prātimokṣa or pātimokkha.

Buddhist Shrine: In Buddhism, a shrine refers to a place where veneration is focused on the Buddha or one of the bodhisattvas.

Site-specific shrines in Buddhism, particularly those that contain relics of deceased buddhas and revered monks, are often designed in the traditional form known as the stupa.

Buddhist Temple: A place of worship for Buddhists, the followers of Buddhism. They include the structures called vihara, chaitya stupa, wat and pagoda in different regions and languages. Traditional Buddhist temples are designed to inspire inner and outer peace.

Carabiner: A carabiner or karabiner is a specialized type of shackle, a metal loop with a spring-loaded gate used to quickly and reversibly connect components, most notably in safety-critical systems.

Catabolism: The set of metabolic pathways that breaks down molecules into smaller units that are either oxidized to release energy or used in other anabolic reactions.

Chai tea: Masala chai is a flavored tea beverage made by brewing black tea with a mixture of aromatic spices, herbs and milk. Originating in the Indian subcontinent, the beverage has gained worldwide popularity, becoming a feature in many coffee and tea houses.

Chengdu Shuangliu International Airport: The major international airport serving Chengdu, the capital of Sichuan province, China. Located about 16 kilometres southwest of downtown Chengdu to the north of Shuangliu District, Shuangliu airport is an important aviation hub for Western China.

Communist Party: In political science, a communist party is a political party that seeks to realize the social and economic goals of Communism through revolution and state policy. The term communist party was popularized by the title of the Manifesto of the Communist Party, by Karl Marx and Friedrich Engels.

Crampons: A crampon is a traction device that is attached to footwear to improve mobility on snow and ice during ice climbing. Besides ice climbing, crampons are also used for secure travel on snow and ice, such as crossing glaciers, snowfields and icefields, ascending snow slopes, and scaling ice-covered rock.

Customs: "Customs" means the Government Service which is responsible for the administration of Customs law and the collection of duties and taxes and which also has the responsibility for the application of other laws and regulations relating to the importation, exportation, movement or storage of goods.

Daddy long-legs spider: Pholcidae, commonly known as cellar spiders, daddy long-legs spider, granddaddy long-legs spider, carpenter spider, daddy long-legger, vibrating spider and skull spider, is a family of araneomorph spiders first described by Ludwig Carl Christian Koch in 1850. It contains over 1800 species divided in 94 genera.

Dal bhat: A traditional meal from the Indian subcontinent, popular in many areas of Nepal, Bangladesh and India. It consists of steamed rice and a cooked lentil soup called dal. It is a staple food in these countries. Bhat or Chawal means "boiled rice" in a number of Indo-Aryan languages.

Dialect: The term dialect (from Latin *dialectus*, *dialectos*, from the Ancient Greek word διάλεκτος, *diálektos*, "discourse", from διά, *diá*, "through" and λέγω, *légō*, "I speak") is used in two distinct ways to refer to two different types of linguistic phenomena: One usage refers to a variety of a language that is a characteristic of a particular group of the language's speakers . . . The other usage of the term "dialect", often deployed in colloquial settings, refers (often somewhat pejoratively) to a language that is socially subordinated to a regional or national standard language, often historically cognate or genetically related to the standard language, but not actually derived *from* the standard language.

Diamox: Acetazolamide, sold under the trade name Diamox, among others, is a medication used to treat glaucoma, epilepsy, altitude sickness, periodic paralysis, idiopathic intracranial hypertension, and heart failure.

Do Sha Tien: Simplified Mandarin pronunciation of "How much?"

Durbar Square: which means Royal Squares in English, is the generic name used to describe plazas and areas opposite the old royal palaces in Nepal.

Everest Base Camp: Everest base camps refers to two base camps on opposite sides of Mount Everest. South Base Camp is in Nepal at an altitude of 5,364 metres, while North Base Camp is in Tibet at 5,150 metres. These camps are rudimentary campsites on Mount Everest that are used by mountain climbers during their ascent and descent.

Frost, Robert: Robert Lee Frost (March 26, 1874 – January 29, 1963) was an American poet. His work was initially published in England before it was published in America.

Glacier: A glacier (US: /ˈɡleɪʃər/ or UK: /ˈɡlæsiər/) is a persistent body of dense ice that is constantly moving under its own weight; it forms where the accumulation of snow exceeds its ablation (melting and sublimation) over many years, often centuries.

Green tea: A type of tea that is made from Camellia synesis leaves and buds that have not undergone the same withering and oxidation process used to make oolong teas and black teas. Green tea originated in China, but its production and manufacture has spread to many other countries in Asia.

Ground Zero: During the September 11, 2001 attacks, two aircraft hijacked by 10 al-Qaeda terrorists flew into the North and

South Towers of the World Trade Center in New York City, causing massive damage and starting fires that caused the weakened 110-story skyscrapers to collapse. The destroyed World Trade Center site soon became known as "ground zero." Rescue workers also used the phrase "The Pile", referring to the pile of rubble that was left after the buildings collapsed.

Guesthouse: A kind of lodging. In some parts of the world (such as for example the Caribbean), guest houses are a type of inexpensive hotel-like lodging. In still others, it is a private home which has been converted for the exclusive use of guest accommodation.

Guide book: A guide book or travel guide is "a book of information about a place designed for the use of visitors or tourists". It will usually include information about sights, accommodation, restaurants, transportation, and activities. Maps of varying detail and historical and cultural information are often included. Different kinds of guide books exist, focusing on different aspects of travel, from adventure travel to relaxation, or aimed at travelers with different incomes, or focusing on sexual orientation or types of diet.

High-altitude cerebral edema (HACE): A medical condition in which the brain swells with fluid because of the physiological effects of traveling to a high altitude. It generally appears in patients who have acute mountain sickness and involves disorientation, lethargy, and nausea among other symptoms.

High-altitude pulmonary edema (HAPE): A life-threatening form of non-cardiogenic pulmonary edema (fluid accumulation in the lungs) that occurs in otherwise healthy mountaineers at altitudes typically above 2,500 meters (8,200 ft).

Hostel: In the Indian subcontinent and South Africa, hostel also refers to boarding schools or student dormitories in resident colleges and universities. In other parts of the world, the word hostel mainly refers to properties offering shared accommodation to travelers or backpackers.

Hunchback of Notre-Dame: (French: Notre-Dame de Paris, lit. 'Our Lady of Paris') is a French Gothic novel by Victor Hugo, published in 1831.

Hurricane: A tropical cyclone is a rapidly rotating storm system characterized by a low-pressure center, a closed low-level atmospheric circulation, strong winds, and a spiral arrangement of thunderstorms that produce heavy rain.

Hurricane Bob: Hurricane Bob (1979) Hurricane Bob was the first Atlantic tropical cyclone to be officially designated using a masculine name after the discontinuation of Joint Army/Navy Phonetic Alphabet names. Less than a day after formation, the system reached tropical storm intensity, followed by hurricane intensity on July 11. The name Bob was used for three tropical cyclones in the Atlantic basin. The name Bob was retired in the spring of 1992, and was replaced by Bill in the 1997 season.

Hurricane Sandy: The deadliest and most destructive hurricane of the 2012 Atlantic hurricane season. Inflicting nearly $70 billion in damage, it was the second-costliest hurricane on record in the United States until surpassed by Hurricanes Harvey and Maria in 2017.

India pale ale: India pale ale is a hoppy beer style within the broader category of pale ale. The term 'pale ale' originally denoted an ale brewed from pale malt. Among the first brewers known to export beer to India was Englishman George Hodgson's Bow Brewery on the Middlesex-Essex border.

Intestinal parasite: An intestinal parasite infection is a condition in which a parasite infects the gastro-intestinal tract of humans and other animals. Such parasites can live anywhere in the body, but most prefer the intestinal wall. Routes of exposure and infection include ingestion of undercooked meat, drinking infected water, fecal-oral transmission and skin absorption. Some types of helminths and protozoa are classified as intestinal parasites that cause infection—those that reside in the intestines. These infections can damage or sicken the host (humans or other animals). If the intestinal parasite infection is caused by helminths, the infection is called helminthiasis.

Jet lag: A physiological condition which results from alterations to the body's circadian rhythms caused by rapid long-distance trans-meridian travel.

JFK International Airport: John F. Kennedy International Airport (IATA: JFK, ICAO: KJFK, FAA LID: JFK) (colloquially referred to as New York-JFK, New York-Kennedy, Kennedy Airport, JFK Airport, JFK or Kennedy) is the primary international airport serving New York City. It is the busiest international air passenger gateway into North America, the 22nd-busiest airport in the world, the sixth-busiest airport in the United States, and the busiest airport in the New York airport system.

Lonely Planet Guidebook: Lonely Planet is a large travel guide book publisher. As of 2011, the company had sold 120 million books since inception and by early 2014, it had sold around 11 million units of its travel apps.

Mandarin: Mandarin is a group of related varieties of Chinese spoken across most of northern and southwestern China. The group includes the Beijing dialect, the basis of Standard Mandarin or Standard Chinese.

Maruti-Suzuki: Maruti Suzuki India Limited, formerly known as Maruti Udyog Limited, is an automobile manufacturer in India.

Momo: Soup momo is a dish with steamed momo immersed in a meat broth. Pan-fried momo is also known as kothey momo. Steamed momo served in hot sauce is called C-momo. There are also a variety of dumplings of Nepal found in the Indian state of Sikkim and Darjeeling district, including tingmo and thaipo.

Mount Everest: Known in Nepali as Sagarmatha and in Tibetan as Chomolungma, is Earth's highest mountain above sea level, located in the Mahalangur Himal sub-range of the Himalayas. The international border between Nepal and China runs across its summit point.

Murray, William James: (born September 21, 1950) is an American actor, comedian, and writer. He first gained exposure on *Saturday Night Live*, a series of performances that earned him his first Emmy Award, and later starred in comedy films including: *Meatballs* (1979), *Caddyshack* (1980), *Stripes* (1981), *Tootsie* (1982), *Ghostbusters* (1984), *Scrooged* (1988), *Ghostbusters II* (1989), *What About Bob?* (1991), and *Groundhog Day* (1993). He also co-directed *Quick Change* (1990).

MythBusters: An Australian-American science entertainment television program created by Peter Rees and produced by Australia's Beyond Television Productions. The series premiered on the Discovery Channel on January 23, 2003.

National Geographic Magazine: National Geographic is the official magazine of the National Geographic Society. It has been published continuously since its first issue in 1888, nine months after the Society itself was founded. It primarily contains articles about science, geography, history, and world culture.

Ne-hao, Ni hao: Simplified Mandarin pronunciation of "Hello."

Pelmeni: Pelmeni are dumplings of Russian cuisine which consist of a filling wrapped in thin, unleavened dough. The debate about the exact place of origin is still active, with Ural and Siberia both maintaining strong claims. Pelmeni are considered as the heart of Russian cuisine.

Privet: Simplified, casual Russian pronunciation of "Hello."

Pyramid International Laboratory-Observatory: Pyramid International Laboratory Observatory near Lobuche.

Roti: A round flatbread native to the Indian subcontinent made from stoneground whole meal flour, traditionally known as atta, and water that is combined into a dough. Roti is consumed in India, Pakistan, Nepal, Sri Lanka, Indonesia, Singapore, Maldives, Thailand, Malaysia and Bangladesh.

Rupee: The common name for the currencies of India, Pakistan, Indonesia, the Maldives, Mauritius, Nepal, Seychelles, and Sri Lanka, and of former currencies of Afghanistan, Tibet, Burma, British East Africa, German East Africa, the Trucial States, and all Gulf Arab Countries (as the Gulf rupee).

Satellite Phone: A satellite telephone, satellite phone or satphone is a type of mobile phone that connects to other phones or the telephone network by radio through orbiting satellites instead of terrestrial cell sites, as cellphones do. The advantage of a satphone is that its use is not limited to areas covered by cell towers; it can be used in most or all geographic locations on the Earth's surface.

Shanghai Pudong International Airport: One of two international airports of Shanghai and a major aviation hub of China. Pudong Airport mainly serves international flights, while the city's other major airport Shanghai Hongqiao International Airport mainly serves domestic and regional flights.

Sherpa: One of the ethnic groups native to the most mountainous regions of Nepal and the Himalayas. The term sherpa or sherwa derives from the Sherpa language words Shar ("east") and Wa ("people"), which refer to their geographical origin in Kham Salmogang of eastern Nepal.

Shrine: A holy or sacred place, which is dedicated to a specific deity, ancestor, hero, martyr, saint, daemon, or similar figure of awe and respect, at which they are venerated or worshipped. Shrines often contain idols, relics, or other such objects associated with the figure being venerated.

SIM card: A subscriber identity module or subscriber identification module, widely known as a SIM card, is an integrated circuit that is intended to securely store the international mobile subscriber identity number and its related key, which are used to identify and authenticate subscribers on mobile telephony devices.

Smart Phone: Smartphones are a class of mobile phones and of multi-purpose mobile computing devices.

Squat toilet: (or squatting toilet) is a toilet used by squatting, rather than sitting. There are several types of squat toilets, but they all consist essentially of a toilet pan or bowl at floor level. Such a toilet pan is also called a "squatting pan". The only exception is a "pedestal" squat toilet, which is of the same height as a sitting toilet. It is in theory also possible to squat over sitting toilets, but this requires extra care to prevent accidents as they are not designed for squatting.

Steripen Freedom: The lightest and smallest water purifier from SteriPEN, the Freedom features an integrated rechargeable battery.

Stone, Angus and Julia: Angus & Julia Stone are an Australian folk and indie pop group, formed in 2006 by brother and sister Angus and Julia Stone. Angus & Julia Stone have released four studio albums: A Book Like This (2007), Down the Way (2010), Angus & Julia Stone (2014), and Snow (2017).

Stupa: (Sanskrit: "heap") A mound-like or hemispherical structure containing relics (such as śarīra – typically the remains of Buddhist monks or nuns) that is used as a place of meditation.

Summit: A point on a surface that is higher in elevation than all points immediately adjacent to it. The topographic terms acme, apex, peak (mountain peak), and zenith are synonymous.

Survivorman: A Canadian-produced television program, broadcast in Canada on the Outdoor Life Network (OLN), and internationally on Discovery Channel and Science Channel.

Swiss Army Knife: A pocketknife or multi-tool manufactured by Victorinox. The term "Swiss Army knife" was coined by American soldiers after World War II due to the difficulty they had in pronouncing "Offiziersmesser", the German name.

Tara Air Pvt. Ltd.: An airline with its head office in Kathmandu, Nepal. It is a subsidiary of Yeti Airlines. Tara Air was formed in 2009 using aircraft from the Yeti Airlines fleet and is based at Tribhuvan International Airport, with secondary hubs at Surkhet and Nepalgunj airports.

Tata bus: Tata Marcopolo (officially Tata Marcopolo Motors Ltd.) is a bus and coach manufacturing company headquartered in Karnataka, India and a joint venture between Tata Motors and Marcopolo S.A.

Tato pani: Simplified Nepali pronunciation of "Hot water."

Therm-A-Rest: Therm-a-Rest is an American outdoor product company specializing in camping mattresses, sleeping bags, camp chairs, hammocks, cots, and pillows.

Tibetan Buddism: The form of Buddhism named after the lands of Tibet where it is the dominant religion. It is also found in the regions surrounding the Himalayas, much of Chinese Central Asia, the Southern Siberian regions such as Tuva, as well as in Mongolia.

Tibetan prayer beads: (or malas, Sanskrit: mālā "garland") A traditional tool used to count. In Tibetan Buddhism, malas of 108 beads are used.

Tibetan prayer flag: A colorful rectangular cloth, often found strung along trails and peaks high in the Himalayas. They are used to bless the surrounding countryside and for other purposes. Prayer flags are believed to have originated with Bon. In Bon, shamanistic Bonpo used primary-colored plain flags in Tibet.

Tibetan prayer wheel: A prayer wheel is a cylindrical wheel on a spindle made from metal, wood, stone, leather or coarse cotton. Traditionally, the mantra Om Mani Padme Hum is written in Newari language of Nepal, on the outside of the wheel.

Tongba: A millet-based alcoholic beverage found in the eastern mountainous region of Nepal and the neighbouring Darjeeling and Sikkim. It is the traditional and indigenous drink of the Limbu people of eastern Nepal. Tongba is culturally and religiously important to the Limbu people of eastern Nepal.

Tour director or guide: A tour guide or a tourist guide is a person who provides assistance, information on cultural, historical and contemporary heritage to people on organized tours and individual clients at educational establishments, religious and historical sites, museums, and at venues of other significant interest, attractions sites.

Trekking: A form of walking, undertaken with the specific purpose of exploring and enjoying the scenery. It usually takes place on trails in areas of relatively unspoiled wilderness. Trekking is a form of walking, undertaken with the specific purpose of exploring and enjoying the scenery.

UNESCO World Heritage Site: A landmark or area which is selected by the United Nations Educational, Scientific and Cultural Organization (UNESCO) as having cultural, historical, scientific or other form of significance, and is legally protected by international treaties.

Wi-Fi: Wi-Fi Alliance is a non-profit organization that promotes Wi-Fi technology and certifies Wi-Fi products for conformity to certain standards of interoperability.

World Wrestling Entertainment, Inc.: d/b/a WWE, is an American integrated media and entertainment company that is primarily known for professional wrestling. WWE has also branched out into other fields, including movies, real estate, and various other business ventures.

Yak: The domestic yak (Bos grunniens) is a long-haired domesticated bovid found throughout the Himalayan region of the Indian subcontinent, the Tibetan Plateau and as far north as Mongolia and Russia. It is descended from the wild yak (Bos mutus).

Yo Kati ho: Simplified Nepali pronunciation of "How much?"

Yuan: The renminbi is the official currency of the People's Republic of China. The yuan is the basic unit of the renminbi, but is also used to refer to the Chinese currency generally, especially in international contexts where "Chinese yuan" is widely used to refer to the renminbi.

Made in the USA
Columbia, SC
10 January 2020

86179538R00117